COPYKAT.COM'S
Dining Out
AT HOME
COOKBOOK

COPYKAT.COM'S *Dining Out* AT HOME COOKBOOK

Recipes for the Most Delicious Dishes from America's Most Popular Restaurants

STEPHANIE MANLEY

Ulysses Press

Published by Ulysses Press
   P.O. Box 3440
   Berkeley, CA 94703
   www.ulyssespress.com

ISBN: 978-1-56975-782-6
Library of Congress Catalog Number 2009940340

Printed in the United States by Bang Printing

10 9 8 7 6 5 4 3 2 1

Acquisitions Editor: Keith Riegert
Managing Editor: Claire Chun
Editor: Lauren Harrison
Proofreader: Sayre Van Young
Production: Judith Metzener
Cover design: Double R Design
Interior design: what!design @ whatweb.com
Interior icons: ©shutterstock.com/Massimo Sairezzo, Harjis A, Seller, Miguel Angel Salinas Salinas, svidenovic, blondinkadesign, Tancha, Mikateke, nata_danilenko
Cover photos: crabcakes ©istockphoto.com/cameronpashak; sliders ©istockphoto.com/dirkr; gingham ©istockphoto.com/Andyd; milkshake ©Getty Images/Hemera Technologies; onion rings ©Getty Images/Hemera Technologies; buffalo wings ©istockphoto.com/kcleine

Distributed by Publishers Group West

To Michael Masterov,
who taught me that limits in life
are the ones you set for yourself.

Contents

Why CopyKat Recipes?   11

Icon Guide   15

DRINKS   16

APPETIZERS   29

SALADS   60

SOUPS   75

MAIN DISHES   93

SIDE DISHES   138

DESSERTS   169

BREAKFASTS   210

SAUCES AND DRESSINGS   227

Conversion Charts   255

Recipe Index   257

Recipe Index by Restaurant   263

About the Author   272

Note to the Reader

CopyKat.com's Dining Out at Home Cookbook is a collection of original recipes created by the author, Stephanie Manley, for the preparation of food items that taste like the ones available from many of America's favorite restaurants and food brands.

All trademarks that appear in recipe titles, ingredient lists, and elsewhere in this book belong to their respective owners and are mentioned here for informational purposes only. Every effort has been made to identify third-party trademarks with the "®" or "™" symbols, as appropriate. No sponsorship or endorsement of this book by, and no affiliation with, the trademark owners is claimed or suggested.

The author encourages her readers to patronize the restaurants and food manufacturers in order to find out for themselves what the authentic versions of these food items taste like!

Why CopyKat Recipes?

Growing up, many years ago, I lived in a very rural area of Texas. Going out to eat at many of the popular restaurants meant a really long drive, so I didn't get the opportunity to dine out very often. I had grown up cooking since I was about four years old. My mom was a brave lady, and she let me take a chair to the stove so I could stand on it and cook. Her comment was, "You would burn yourself a lot, but I figured you would eventually stop that." Once I started cooking, I never stopped.

My whole fascination with "copy cat" recipes really began with a trip to the Olive Garden®. I never had Alfredo sauce before, and honestly, for me that moment was life-changing. I thought Alfredo sauce was the most decadent pasta sauce imaginable, creamy and rich, with a hint of garlic. I wanted to re-create that sauce, and I was a woman on a mission. In high school and college, I worked at several different restaurants, and unlike most kids, I read cookbooks instead of novels. In 1995, when I was in college, I created a web page and used it to put up my family recipes and a few "copy cat" recipes as well. Guess what everyone was interested in? Well, it wasn't my grandmother's pecan pie recipe (which, by the way, is spectacular). Ever since then I have been creating original copy-cat recipes for the Internet, and I have loved every minute of it. I now have about 1500 recipes online, most of which are of the restaurant variety, while others are some of my personal favorites, and you can still find my family's recipes online as well.

So people always ask me, why do you make these recipes? I tell them that I love going out to eat, but you know, I can't always afford to or even have the time to go out as much as I would like. Making your own restaurant-style recipes at home doesn't take away from your dining experience at all. At home, you may be able to cook with your friends or your family, which you obviously can't do when you go out to eat. And dining at home means you can combine menu items that you would never be able to get out at a restaurant. Personally, I enjoy making a salad dressing from Sweet Tomatoes®, combining it with my favorite pasta dish from the Olive Garden®, and finishing with a dessert from The Cheesecake Factory®. Now you can't do that in a restaurant!

Another advantage of cooking at home is cost savings. Restaurants often operate on a method where they know how much of each dollar on a menu is for the food costs, and the rest of each dollar taken in is spent on operating costs. Well, at home, our economic situation isn't quite the same: What we spend on food is how much it costs. For example, Cinnabon® Cinnamon Rolls, which in my personal opinion are dropped down from heaven, retail for just under four dollars each. I can show you how to make a whole pan of them for less than ten dollars. Watching when items go on sale at the grocery store and menu planning around those sale items only increases that dramatic cost savings.

So I will be totally honest with you: If you set something down in front of me, I am likely to eat all of it. It doesn't matter if it is a supersized plate of pasta or a normal portion. In a restaurant, I can't control what portion I am given. Sure, I could be good and divide my portion in half and take half home, but what is more likely is that I'll eat everything and not take anything home. When I cook at home, I can portion out what I am going to eat. For me, this is a big advantage—often restaurant food contains more fat, salt, and sugar than we should consume according to modern dietary guidelines. Being able to control what I put on the plate really helps me.

I also like to modify my recipes slightly when I make them. When I write the recipes, I create them as closely as I can to the restaurant versions, but when I make them for myself, I'll make modifications. For example, I generally add more garlic and onions than the recipe normally calls for because I love garlic and onions (in fact, I love garlic so much that in case there is an invasion of vampires, I am certain to be safe). I also may add less salt or make a sugar substitution. Knowing how a recipe is made helps you to make better decisions for modifying it.

Another question I often hear is, how do you choose which recipes you will re-create? I often get my inspiration from people just like you. Creating and sharing recipes with people online is a passion of mine. I love the interaction that is there, and I love the fact that so many readers have offered suggestions on what recipes to re-create. I also choose recipes based upon a few other things, like how well-known the restaurant is that serves a particular recipe. For example, there's a hamburger joint where I live called Bill's Café. I love Bill's Café, and it has some of the best burgers around, but chances are you don't know about that place, so it probably won't make it onto the website. I also choose recipes that are made with what I call "real food," and by that I mean I like to re-create recipes that are minus artificial thickening agents, spice blends with a lot of unknown preservatives, and ingredients that I can't readily identify (and trust me, I can identify a lot of food).

So you aren't going to see me even try to duplicate recipes for dry chicken soup mixes, bouillon cubes, and/or other unique items like this. I also can't re-create a recipe once it's been discontinued, although I get a lot of requests for these items. I know we never really know when a menu item is going to be removed from a restaurant's menu, and quite a few of the recipes in this book have been taken off a restaurant's current offerings, but I really can't try to make something that I have never tasted.

You might wonder why I think I can re-create recipes so well. In addition to cooking for a few restaurants, I have done my share of cooking for charity events and for other large catering-types of events—one time my best friend talked me into cooking out at a rustic campsite, and we made a meal for 200 people that had four courses with multiple dishes for each course. I also test out my recipes in many different ways. First, I try the recipe at a restaurant several different times. A recipe can be prepared different ways, by different cooks. Should this happen? No, but I have noticed slight variations each time the dish is served. I test out all my recipes many times. Once, I made a dish eighteen times before I got it to where I liked it (needless to say, it was years before I wanted another chocolate chip muffin). Also, since I post the recipes online and literally have thousands of people visiting to the site each and every day, I receive feedback from readers. On occasion, recipes have been modified to make them more authentic.

Using ingredients that are common to your average grocery store is something I try to keep in mind. I have lived where the grocery stores don't offer a wide selection of items. For those who live in major metropolitan areas, that may not seem like a big deal, but for those of us who live in more rural places, well, it is often a painful realization that you can't make a special dish because your local store doesn't even carry what you need.

Included in this book is a sampling of the recipes you will find online at CopyKat.com, and this book really should be called *Best of CopyKat.com*. Here you have the most tried-and-true recipes. They have been tested and retested by people just like you. I hope you enjoy my restaurant re-creations, so you too can enjoy dining out at home.

Icon Guide

AUTHOR FAVORITE

COCKTAIL PARTY

DINNER FOR ONE

DINNER FOR TWO

IMPRESS THE GUEST

MAKE AHEAD

MEAT LOVERS

QUICK AND EASY

SPICY

TAILGATING

VEGETARIAN

Drinks

×××××××××××××××××××××××××××××××

One of my favorite things to order when I go out is a drink. Around the house I normally just open up a can of soda or even make a glass of iced tea. Making unusual drinks can be a wonderful way to enhance a meal or an evening.

You may want to have a few cocktail glasses on hand, and they don't need to be fancy—you can find inexpensive ones anywhere. The two types I recommend having are highball glasses and old-fashioned glasses. The highball glasses are perfect for iced tea and any other drinks that go in tall glasses. Highballs typically hold about 8 to 12 ounces, and old-fashioned glasses hold about 6 to 10 ounces. You may also want to pick up a cocktail shaker, but if you don't have one, you can also use two glasses you have around the house (one needs to be larger than the other) or you can mix drinks in a large glass. Making a fun drink really is a wonderful way to make any occasion extra special.

Marshmallow Rice Krispies® Shake

The first time I heard of this, I wondered how good a shake with Rice Krispies® could be. Well, I was surprised because this shake is really good. Jack in the Box® is known for tasty and inventive fast food, and this shake definitely fits the bill. They use premium ice cream, so I suggest that you use a good-quality brand, as well. A couple of good brands that I have used are the Blue Bell® homemade vanilla ice cream or Blue Bunny vanilla ice cream.

1 tablespoon Marshmallow Fluff

2 tablespoons milk

1 cup vanilla ice cream

2 tablespoons Rice Krispies

In a small bowl or glass, combine the Marshmallow Fluff and the milk—if you don't combine these two first, it is really hard to get the fluff to mix properly into the ice cream. Scoop the ice cream into a large glass and add the milk mixture. Stir until it reaches the consistency you desire. You can use a blender to do this if you want. Use a spoon to stir in the Rice Krispies just before serving.

YIELD: 1 SERVING, 1½ CUPS

Secret Passion Punch

This restaurant has a fun, festive, beachlike atmosphere. Jeans and T-shirts are the perfect attire there. This punch is a light and fruity punch. One warning though: Don't have too many of these. They don't taste strong, but drinking too many will sneak up on you.

^{1}/$_3$ cup canned pineapple juice

^{2}/$_3$ cup cranberry juice cocktail

2 ounces light rum

1 ounce crème de banana liqueur

1 ounce Chambord
(raspberry liqueur)

chipped ice

maraschino cherries, for garnish

orange wedges, for garnish

Stir the pineapple juice, cranberry juice cocktail, rum, crème de banana, and Chambord together in a large glass. Pour the mixture over the chipped ice in two highball glasses. Garnish each glass with a maraschino cherry and a wedge of orange.

YIELD: 2 (6-OUNCE) SERVINGS

Ya Ya Punch

★ 🍸 🕐

One of my favorite recipes to make at a party is this Ya Ya Punch. A variety of fruit flavors make this drink popular with many people, and it's good to make at a cocktail party because people typically have rum and vodka on hand. The two fruit juices can also be used in many other cocktails.

1 cup canned pineapple juice

1 cup cranberry juice (cranapple juice is also good in this)

1 ounce vodka

1 ounce peach schnapps

1 ounce coconut rum

splash of grenadine

Stir all the ingredients together in a small pitcher and pour them over ice in highball glasses.

YIELD: 3 (6-OUNCE) SERVINGS

CopyKat.com's KAHLÚA®

Mudslide

You don't have to buy the premixed bottles at the store—you can make this at home and adjust the drink for your own personal taste. In fact, I would *rather* make Mudslides at home. That way I can switch the regular vodka for vanilla vodka for enhanced flavor.

½ ounce Kahlúa	1 ounce milk
½ ounce Bailey's Irish Cream	ice
½ ounce vodka	

Pour the Kahlúa, Irish Cream, vodka, and milk into a shaker and shake well. Pour the mixture into an old-fashioned glass and add ice.

YIELD: 1 SERVING

CopyKat.com's **RED ROBIN®**

Freckled Lemonade

Red Robin® restaurants are fantastic places to get burgers with creative toppings. I like my burger with a side of bottomless french fries and this thirst-quenching beverage, which combines lemonade and frozen strawberries. You can find cartons of frozen strawberries with syrup in the freezer section of most grocery stores.

> 2 tablespoons frozen strawberries with syrup, thawed
> 1½ cups cold fresh lemonade
> ice

In a tall highball glass, pour in the lemonade and add ice to raise the level of lemonade to about 1½ inches from the top of the glass. Carefully spoon the thawed strawberries on top of the lemonade and gently stir.

YIELD: 1 SERVING

CopyKat.com's **RUBY TUESDAY™**

Smurf Punch

Remember Smurfs from Saturday morning cartoons? You can make a drink that looks just like them. This non-alcoholic punch is perfect for the kids.

ice (optional)	whipped cream
½ cup lemon-lime soda or ginger ale	maraschino cherry
2 to 3 drops blue food coloring	

Fill a tall glass with ice, if using, and lemon-lime soda or ginger ale. Add the blue food coloring. Top with whipped cream and a cherry.

YIELD: 1 SERVING

CopyKat.com's **SOGGY DOLLAR BAR™**

Painkiller

★ 🍸 ⏱

If you like fruity drinks, you will enjoy this one. It is like a piña colada without all of the work. The Soggy Dollar Bar™ is located in the Virgin Islands and has been around since the 1970s. I am told the restaurant got its name because everyone came up to the counter with soggy dollars to order their drinks. Now, we all can't make it out there to enjoy this fine bar, but you can make one of their cocktails at home and pretend you're there. I generally make Painkillers in multiples, because if you give someone a taste of this, you will often lose your drink.

2 ounces dark rum
(I like Pusser's)

1 ounce coconut cream liqueur

4 ounces canned pineapple juice

1 ounce orange juice

ice

nutmeg, for garnish

Shake the rum, coconut cream, pineapple juice, and orange juice in a shaker and pour the mixture over ice in a highball or tall glass. Sprinkle nutmeg on top and serve.

YIELD: 1 SERVING

Cherry Limeade

★ ⏱

Nothing is quite as refreshing as a Cherry Limeade. This recipe was introduced to me by my friend Russ Stevens. When we were in college together, he claimed it was the best thing to help him get through a long day. College may have ended long ago, but I still crave these once in a while. You can also make the diet version by substituting your favorite flavor of diet lemon-lime soda.

2 tablespoons cherry syrup (see note)	ice
¹/₃ of a lime	maraschino cherry (optional)
1 (12-ounce) can lemon-lime soda	

Add the cherry syrup to a tall glass. Juice the lime into the glass and then put it in. Pour in the lemon-lime soda and add enough ice to fill the glass ²/₃ full. If you like, you can add a maraschino cherry.

NOTE: Many grocery stores carry the cherry syrup in the ice cream section. I have also spotted it where drink mixers are sold. You can substitute grenadine for cherry syrup, but it will give a slightly bitter flavor.

YIELD: 1 SERVING

CopyKat.com's

Sweet Tea ✓

One of the requests I have gotten over the years is how to make sweet tea just like a restaurant does. It isn't difficult to do, but you have to keep a few things in mind: Keep your pitcher clean, because otherwise tea can get old and develop a moldy taste. Also, be sure not to steep your tea too long, or it may become bitter. Good brands of tea to use in this recipe are Luzianne™ or Lipton®.

2 cups boiling water	ice
4 small (or 2 family-sized) bags black tea	cool water
½ cup sugar	

Pour the boiling water into a 2-quart pitcher. Add the tea bags and allow them to steep for 3 minutes only (if the tea bags are left in longer, the tea may become bitter). Remove the tea bags and stir in the sugar, mixing it completely. You may want to adjust the amount of sugar. Fill the pitcher with ice and then add cool water.

YIELD: APPROXIMATELY 1½ QUARTS

CopyKat.com's **SWISS MISS™**

Cocoa Mix

What could warm you up more on a cold evening than a cup of cocoa? You don't need to buy individually packaged cocoa mix, and you can make this for much less. Put this mix in a jar and wrap it with a bow to make a pretty gift.

> 1 (16-ounce) box nonfat dry milk
>
> 1 cup sugar
>
> ¾ cup cocoa powder

Sift all the ingredients together three times. Store this mixture in a tightly sealed container in a cool place. When ready to use, add a couple of heaping tablespoons to hot water.

YIELD: 10 SERVINGS

CopyKat.com's **T.G.I. FRIDAY'S®**

One Hour in the Candy Store

T.G.I. Friday's® has a constantly changing and creative menu—I know they will always have something new and tasty. This sweet, creamy dessert drink is sheer heaven.

1 ounce Chambord (raspberry liqueur)

1 ounce crème de noyaux

1 ounce amaretto (almond liqueur)

2 scoops vanilla ice cream

1 cup crushed ice

3 Oreo cookies

6 maraschino cherries, stems removed

In a blender, combine the Chambord, crème de noyaux, amaretto, vanilla ice cream, and ice and blend until smooth. Add the Oreos and pulse the blender a few times. Pour into a glass and top with cherries.

YIELD: 1 SERVING

Sex on the Beach

Try our version of this fruity and refreshing drink.

¾ ounce vodka

¾ ounce Midori (melon liqueur)

¾ ounce Chambord (raspberry liqueur)

1½ ounces canned pineapple juice

1½ ounces cranberry juice

ice

Pour the vodka, melon liqueur, raspberry liqueur, pineapple juice, and cranberry juice into a shaker and shake well. Pour the mixture into an old-fashioned glass and add ice.

YIELD: 1 SERVING

Appetizers

A ppetizers are wonderful additions to any meal. I really judge a restaurant by their creativity when it comes to their appetizers, and I can be won over by tasty starters. We all have our usual standard dishes at our favorite restaurants, but just before the meal, we can let our hair down and enjoy a variety of items, and many restaurants really pull out all the stops when it comes to inventive appetizers.

You can use many of the starters here at a potluck, or even bring them to your next tailgating party. You can also make whole meals out of a couple of appetizers, or throw a cocktail party with several different dishes. For fun, you may want to find some inexpensive small plates at the bargain bin at your favorite stores, farmers markets, or even thrift shops. Serve up a couple of different appetizers on crazy plates, and make the gathering fun and festive.

CopyKat.com's ALMOND ROCA®
Gourmet Popcorn

When I spotted this in a specialty food store, I had to buy it. Caramel popcorn is delicious, but this is better. The buttery toffee flavor and the crunchy almonds taste wonderful together. If you have never made this style of popcorn, you should give it a try—you don't know what you're missing!

3 quarts (12 cups) popped popcorn, plain

½ cup brown sugar

½ cup sugar

½ cup butter

½ teaspoon salt

½ cup light corn syrup

¼ teaspoon baking soda

1½ tablespoons butter flavoring

1 (5-ounce) bag sliced almonds

Place the popped popcorn in a large roasting pan that has been sprayed with a nonstick spray and set aside. In a saucepan on low heat, mix the brown sugar, sugar, butter, salt, and corn syrup. Let the mixture come to a soft boil and then place a lid on the pan for 30 seconds. Remove the lid and stir with a clean spoon so that all the sugar and salt crystals are dissolved and none get back in the mixture. Turn the heat down and let the mixture boil gently without a lid for 5 minutes, stirring constantly. Preheat the oven to 225°F. When 5 minutes are up, remove the pan from the heat and mix in the baking soda. The syrup will foam, but this is normal. Stir until the baking soda is completely dissolved. Add the butter flavoring and stir some more. Pour the syrup over the popcorn, slowly stirring the popcorn constantly to gently coat it. When the popcorn is coated, pour the almonds in and stir well. Bake the popcorn for 1 hour. Stir and mix the popcorn every 15 minutes. When the popcorn is finished baking, pour it onto a nonstick surface to cool. Plastic wrap works well for this and is easy to clean up.

YIELD: 12 SERVINGS

CopyKat.com's **APPLEBEE'S®**

Pico de Gallo

Pico de gallo is a wonderful accompaniment to many dishes because it's low in fat and can be made spicy or mild. You can use this relish on quesadillas, eggs, tacos, or you may want to serve it with corn chips.

3 cups diced tomatoes

1 cup diced onion

2 tablespoons finely diced jalapeño peppers

½ cup minced cilantro

2 teaspoons salt

½ teaspoon black pepper

½ teaspoon garlic powder

1 tablespoon lemon juice

If you want a less-spicy salsa, remove the seeds from the jalapeño peppers when you dice them. Combine all the ingredients together in a bowl and stir well. This is best when left to sit for 2 hours or overnight.

YIELD: APPROXIMATELY 4 CUPS

CopyKat.com's **APPLEBEE'S®**

Quesadillas

No one can match the taste of Applebee's® quesadillas, but this CopyKat version comes pretty close. Be sure to serve these with your favorite guacamole and sour cream.

2 slices lean bacon, cut into ½-inch pieces

1 tablespoon Applebee's Pico de Gallo (page 31)

2 tablespoons softened butter

2 (8-inch) flour tortillas

¼ cup shredded Colby Jack cheese

guacamole

sour cream

picante sauce

Fry the sliced bacon in a frying pan on medium heat until it starts to turn crisp but not hard and brittle. Remove the bacon from the pan, drain it on a paper towel, and set aside. Prepare the Applebee's Pico de Gallo according to the recipe directions. Preheat a nonstick frying pan on medium heat. Spread butter lightly on one side of each tortilla. Place the buttered side of one tortilla down in the hot pan. Sprinkle 2 tablespoons of bacon over the entire tortilla, then add the pico de gallo and Jack cheese over the bacon. Place the second tortilla on top of the fixings, buttered side up. Cook for 1 to 2 minutes, just long enough to heat the inside ingredients, and then carefully flip the quesadilla over on the other side and finish cooking. The quesadilla should be heated through but not browned. Remove the quesadilla from the pan, place it on a serving dish, and cut it into individual triangle pieces. Serve with your favorite guacamole, sour cream, and picante sauce.

YIELD: 1 SERVING

CopyKat.com's **BENNIGAN'S™** ✓

Potato Wedges

This is a really inexpensive recipe that's fun for a party because you can assemble the potato wedges ahead of time and warm them up when you are ready to serve them. I like to bring these to a tailgating party. You can the enjoy hulled-out potatoes as mashed potatoes later.

4 medium Idaho baking potatoes	1 bunch green onions, diced
½ cup shredded Colby cheese	½ cup sour cream
4 tablespoons Real Bacon Bits	

Preheat the oven to 350°F. Wash the potatoes well, score them with a knife, piercing the skin of the potato at least four times about 1-inch apart, and bake for 1 hour. Remove the potatoes from the oven and allow them to cool so that you can handle them.

When the potatoes are cool, cut them in half and scoop out the "meat" of the potato. Be sure to leave at least ¼ inch of meat on the skin. Spray a baking dish with cooking spray and place the hollowed-out halves in the pan. Sprinkle the potatoes with the cheese and bacon bits. Place the potatoes in a 350°F oven for 5 to 10 minutes or until the cheese has melted. Remove the potatoes from the oven. Sprinkle the green onions on top and serve with sour cream.

YIELD: 4 SERVINGS, 8 WEDGES

Awesome Blossom®

Our version of this recipe has that wonderful flavor of Chili's®, but if you want something a little less challenging to fry up, you can cut your onion into strips or even rings to make this recipe a little easier. You may want to experiment on your own with creative ways to use these crispy fried battered onions.

2½ cups flour	1 large Vidalia onion
2 teaspoons seasoned salt	10 cups vegetable oil
½ teaspoon coarsely ground pepper	1 cup buttermilk
¼ teaspoon garlic powder	

Mix the flour, seasoned salt, pepper, and garlic powder together in a bowl. Slice the onion like a blossom by cutting off the top quarter (the part with the stem). Then peel the onion, being very careful to leave the root intact. Carefully slice through the middle of the onion from the top flat part down, but stop about half an inch before you get to the root, taking care not to cut through it. In the same way, slice the rest of the onion like a pie into many servings. Then soak the onion in cold ice water for 30 minutes so its "petals" will start to open up.

In a large pot or your deep-fryer, heat the oil to approximately 350°F. Drain the onion upside down on paper towels, then dip it in the flour mixture and coat it well; the flour should be all the way inside the petals. Dip the onion in the buttermilk, and then back in the flour mixture. Place the onion in the hot oil and fry it until golden. The oil should cover the onion. When the onion is done, drain it well, place it on a plate, and cut out the center so the petals can easily be removed.

YIELD: 4 TO 6 SERVINGS

CopyKat.com's **CHILI'S®**

Salsa

Making salsa isn't hard, and it is less expensive and tastes great when you make it fresh. You can use this with thin crispy corn chips for appetizers, or with your favorite tacos. I have even used leftover salsa when making homemade chili.

1 tablespoon plus 1 teaspoon canned jalapeño peppers, diced (not pickled)

¼ cup yellow onion, diced

1 (14½-ounce) can tomatoes and green chilies

1 (14½-ounce) can whole peeled tomatoes, and their juices

½ to ¾ teaspoon garlic salt

¼ teaspoon sugar

½ teaspoon cumin

Place the jalapeños and onions in a food processor and process for just a few seconds. You only want to chop the onions and jalapeños coarsely so they have lots of shape; if they process too long you will have a paste. Add the tomatoes with green chilies, the whole peeled tomatoes, and the garlic salt, sugar, and cumin. Process all the ingredients until well blended, but do not purée them. Transfer the salsa to a covered container and refrigerate. A couple of hours of chilling will help blend and enrich the flavor.

YIELD: APPROXIMATELY 4 CUPS

CopyKat.com's **CHILI'S®**

Skillet Queso

This is a wonderful cheese dip, perfect for any tailgating party. It reheats very well, so it can be made ahead of time and reheated when you are ready. I don't always specify brands, but here you'll get the best results with Velveeta® processed cheese and Hormel® brand chili.

> 2 pounds Velveeta
> (pasteurized processed cheese)
> 2 (15-ounce) cans Hormel Chili, no beans

Slice the cheese into large cubes and place them in an electric crock pot turned on low heat. Add the cans of chili and allow the cheese to melt, then mix the cheese and chili together well. You can also heat the cheese and chili together in the microwave in a large bowl. Microwave them for 1 minute on high, stir, and repeat until the cheese melts.

YIELD: APPROXIMATELY 8 CUPS

Guacamole

Guacamole is a staple of Tex-Mex food, and you can enjoy this tasty dip anytime.

6 ripe avocados

⅓ cup minced red onion

1 jalapeño pepper, minced

1 clove garlic, minced

2 tablespoons freshly squeezed lime juice

salt

Cut the avocados in half, scoop out the "meat" into a large bowl, and gently break them into smaller pieces, but leave them very chunky. Add the red onion, jalapeño, garlic, and lime juice. Mix the ingredients together and salt to your desired taste.

   NOTE: If you don't like the heat of a jalapeno pepper, remove the seeds when you mince the pepper, because that's where the heat is carried.

YIELD: APPROXIMATELY 2 CUPS

CopyKat.com's CRUNCH 'N MUNCH™

Toffee Pretzels

Looking for something different? Do you like toffee popcorn? If you enjoy salty-sweet treats, you'll love these inexpensive pretzels covered in a crunchy, buttery candy coating.

10 cups pretzels, salted (pretzel-shaped, not sticks)	¼ teaspoon salt
½ cup light corn syrup	½ cup butter
½ cup sugar	¼ teaspoon baking soda
½ cup brown sugar	3 tablespoons liquid butter flavoring

Spray a large baking pan with a nonstick spray, pour in the pretzels, and set aside. In a saucepan over low heat, combine the corn syrup, sugar, brown sugar, salt, and butter and mix well. When the mixture is melted and starts to bubble lightly, place a lid on the pan for 30 seconds. After 30 seconds, remove the lid and stir with a clean spoon to help prevent any sugar or salt crystals from getting back into the syrup mixture. Turn the temperature down and let the syrup boil gently for 5 minutes, stirring frequently. When the mixture has cooked for 5 minutes, remove it from the heat, add the baking soda, and stir. Make sure all the baking soda has been mixed through; the sugar will foam and this is normal. Add the butter flavoring and stir well. Pour the hot toffee syrup over the pretzels. Stir, making sure all the pretzels are coated.

Preheat the oven to 225°F and bake the pretzels for 1 hour, stirring every 15 minutes to coat them with the toffee mixture. When they're finished baking, remove the pretzels from the oven and pour them onto a nonstick surface. Plastic wrap works well for this and is easy to clean up.

YIELD: APPROXIMATELY 12 CUPS

Spinach Artichoke Dip

Houston's™ is known for their fine dining and high-quality food, and their chefs pay attention to small details. Filled with a variety of cheeses, artichokes, spinach, and more, this dish has a lot of finesse and will impress even your most discerning guests.

1 (6¼-ounce) jar marinated artichokes, drained

⅓ cup freshly grated Romano cheese

½ teaspoon minced garlic

¼ cup freshly grated Parmesan cheese

1 (10-ounce) package frozen chopped spinach, thawed and drained very well

⅓ cup cream or half-and-half

½ cup sour cream

1 cup shredded mozzarella cheese

Preheat the oven to 350°F. In a food processor, blend the artichokes, Romano cheese, garlic, and Parmesan cheese for about 1 to 1½ minutes. The artichokes and cheeses should be minced, but should not be pasty.

In a mixing bowl, combine the drained spinach, cream, sour cream, and mozzarella cheese, and stir well. To this mixture add in the ingredients from the food processor. Spray a shallow ovenproof 1-quart serving dish with nonstick cooking spray. Pour the artichoke mixture into the baking dish and bake for 20 to 25 minutes. When the artichoke dip is removed from the oven it should be a little bubbly and the cheese should be melted through. Serve with your favorite heated tortilla chips, sour cream, and salsa and enjoy.

YIELD: 4 TO 6 SERVINGS

Crab Dip

This was a recipe requested by many visitors to the CopyKat.com website. I have found that when so many people inquire about a recipe, that means I should go and try the dish, and I am always amazed that I have missed something so incredible tasting. Joe's Crab Shack™ uses a lot of fresh seafood, but with this dish you can easily make a tasty crab dip with canned crab meat.

2 ounces cream cheese, softened

1 tablespoon mayonnaise

¼ cup sour cream

1 tablespoon butter, softened

¼ teaspoon seasoned salt

⅛ teaspoon paprika

4 teaspoons diced yellow onion

1 (6-ounce) can crab meat, drained

4 teaspoons finely diced green bell pepper

¼ cup shredded mozzarella cheese

freshly diced green onion, for garnish

freshly chopped parsley, for garnish

Preheat the oven to 350°F. With an electric mixer, mix the cream cheese, mayonnaise, sour cream, and butter in a medium bowl until smooth. Blend in the seasoned salt and paprika. Stir in the yellow onions, crab meat, green bell pepper, and mozzarella cheese. Transfer the mixture to a lightly greased, small, shallow baking dish and bake until the dip bubbles, about 10 to 14 minutes. Garnish with green onion and parsley and serve with unsalted or very lightly salted corn chips. This appetizer makes a great light lunch with a crisp salad.

YIELD: 4 TO 6 SERVINGS

Stuffed Jalapeños

★ ▯ ⬭

These peppers are so good you won't be able to stop eating them. I like to make these for a holiday party, or even a potluck, and I never have any left over. The cream cheese takes away the heat of the jalapeño peppers, so you get some heat, but not too much.

1 (8-ounce) package cream cheese, softened	1 tablespoon minced pimiento peppers (from a jar)
¼ cup mayonnaise	1 (26-ounce) can whole pickled jalapeño peppers, sliced in half lengthwise and seeds removed
2 tablespoons dried chives	

Whip the softened cream cheese with an electric mixer, then add the mayonnaise, chives, and pimientos. Blend the filling until it's smooth and fluffy and the sour cream and cream cheese are well blended. Fill the jalapeños with the cream cheese mixture. Cover and store the jalapeños in the refrigerator until you are ready to enjoy them.

◇◇◇

YIELD: APPROXIMATELY 40 PEPPERS

Tex-Mex Queso

Queso is a standard at many Tex-Mex restaurants, but Monterey's™ makes theirs a little differently. They use green chilies and onions for the added flavor. My suggestion here is to use two different brands of pasteurized processed cheese—Velveeta® imparts a unique flavor, but using it alone doesn't give you the right flavor.

½ a medium onion, chopped fine

1 tablespoon butter

1 pound Velveeta

1 pound generic-brand pasteurized processed cheese

1 (4-ounce) can diced green chilies

In a large saucepan, sauté the onions and butter over medium heat until the onions become clear. Cut the Velveeta and the generic-brand cheese into cubes and add them to the saucepan. When the cheeses are melted, add the green chilies and heat until everything is well heated. This is also tasty reheated.

YIELD: 6 CUPS

CopyKat.com's NAN'S™

Ham and Swiss Spirals

Spirals, rolled-up tortillas with filling, are a fun and easy addition to a party, and these are especially good with a very flavorful cream cheese filling using spinach and a hint of spice. These nice little finger foods stay fresh longer than traditional finger sandwiches and can be made a day or two ahead of time and served when you are ready to entertain.

8 ounces cream cheese, softened

¼ cup mayonnaise

1 tablespoon brown mustard

1½ teaspoons prepared horseradish

¼ teaspoon salt

1½ teaspoons roasted garlic

¼ teaspoon sugar

10 large (10- to 12-inch) flour tortillas

1 (10-ounce) package frozen spinach, thawed, rinsed, and completely drained of all liquid

10 thin ham slices

10 slices Swiss cheese (same size as the ham)

pickles (optional), for garnish

cherry tomatoes (optional), for garnish

With an electric mixer, whip the cream cheese, then add the mayonnaise, mustard, horseradish, salt, garlic, and sugar and blend until the mixture is uniform in texture. Spread the cream cheese mixture on the tortillas, about 3 tablespoons each, depending on the size. Sprinkle 2 tablespoons per tortilla of spinach on top of the cheese spread. Place one slice of ham near the edge of each tortilla and then put a slice of Swiss cheese on top of the ham. Roll the tortillas around the ham and cheese. Wrap the rolls in plastic, and let them set in the refrigerator for several hours. The rolls may be made the day before and be kept in the refrigerator for several days if sealed. When the rolls have set and keep their shape, cut them into ¼-inch slices. Arrange them on a tray and garnish with pickles or cherry tomatoes.

YIELD: 50 PIECES

Red Hot Sauce

Ninfa's™, a restaurant in the Houston area, is known for their superfresh salsa. This salsa is easy to prepare, tastes so good, and should be enjoyed immediately.

5 pounds fresh, ripe, whole tomatoes, cored (do not peel)

4 fresh jalapeño peppers

2 tablespoons oil (vegetable, olive, or lard)

½ a large yellow onion, chopped

6 cloves garlic

2 ounces fresh cilantro, chopped

Preheat the oven to 400°F. Place the cored whole tomatoes and whole jalapeños in a shallow pan, like a rimmed cookie sheet, in a single layer. Roast for 30 minutes until the tomatoes and jalapeños are charred. They will be black, but that is what takes away the acidity and gives them a roasted flavor. You don't have to turn them while they're roasting.

While the tomatoes and jalapeños are roasting, heat the oil in a pan and sauté the onion and garlic until it's transparent, then let cool.

After the tomatoes and jalapeños are roasted, place all the ingredients (except for the cilantro) in a blender, leaving the tomatoes and jalapeños whole, and blend for about 15 seconds, taking care not to overblend or the mixture will be too watery. You may have to do this in several batches if you don't have a commercial-sized blender. Roughly chop the cilantro and add it to the sauce. You can also vary the amount of jalapeños or garlic to your taste.

YIELD: APPROXIMATELY 6 CUPS

Fried Mozzarella

★ 🫛

Fried mozzarella is so tasty and can be expensive, but by using packaged Italian-seasoned bread crumbs you can make it at home for less. You can serve this freshly prepared fried mozzarella with your favorite marinara or spaghetti sauce.

8 cups vegetable oil

1 (16-ounce) package mozzarella cheese

2 eggs, beaten

¼ cup water

1½ cups Italian seasoned bread crumbs

½ teaspoon garlic salt

1 teaspoon Italian seasoning

⅔ cup flour

⅓ cup cornstarch

In a large pot or your deep-fryer, heat the vegetable oil to 350°F. If your mozzarella cheese is in a brick, slice it into about ³/₈-inch slices and then cut the slices crossways to make triangles. Beat the eggs with the water and set aside. Mix the bread crumbs, garlic salt, and Italian seasoning and set aside. Mix the flour with the cornstarch and set aside. Dip each cheese triangle in the flour mixture, then in the egg wash, and then coat them with bread crumbs. Carefully place each triangle in the hot oil and fry until golden—this takes just a few seconds, so watch carefully. When the cheese pieces are golden, remove them from the hot oil with a slotted spoon and drain. Serve with your favorite Italian sauce and enjoy.

YIELD: 4 TO 6 SERVINGS

Hot Artichoke Dip

This is a favorite dip at the Olive Garden®, and you can make it ahead of when you will need it and serve it when you are ready to enjoy. I like dishes like this because by making this ahead of time, you won't be rushed when you have friends over, and you'll be able to spend time with your guests rather than in the kitchen.

1 (8-ounce) package light cream cheese, room temperature (I like the light texture better, but regular is fine)

¼ cup mayonnaise (do not use Miracle Whip)

¼ cup Parmesan cheese

¼ cup Romano cheese (or an extra ¼ cup Parmesan)

1 clove garlic, finely minced

½ teaspoon dry basil (or 1 tablespoon fresh)

¼ teaspoon garlic salt

1 (14-ounce) can marinated artichoke hearts, drained, coarsely chopped

½ cup chopped spinach, frozen or steamed, drained well

salt and pepper, to taste

¼ cup shredded mozzarella cheese

Cream together the cream cheese, mayonnaise, Parmesan cheese, Romano cheese, garlic, basil, and garlic salt. Mix well. Add the artichoke hearts and drained spinach, and mix until blended. Season with salt and pepper to your desired taste. If you aren't serving it right away, store the dip in a covered container until you are ready to use.

Preheat the oven to 350°F. Spray a pie pan with nonstick cooking spray, pour in the dip, and top with the mozzarella cheese. Bake for 25 minutes or until the top is browned. Serve with toasted bread.

YIELD: 4 SERVINGS

San Remo Dip

By using a few ingredients you'll find in your pantry, you can make this popular dip that's brimming with seafood. It should be served with breadsticks, but any sort of crusty bread will do, and any leftovers go very well on pasta.

2 tablespoons olive oil

2 tablespoons flour

1 (6-ounce) can tiny shrimp

1 (6-ounce) can crab meat

2 ounces cream cheese, room temperature, cubed

1/4 teaspoon salt

1/8 teaspoon crushed garlic

1 teaspoon prepared horseradish

1/3 cup shredded Asiago cheese

1/4 cup plus 2 tablespoons freshly and finely shredded Parmesan cheese, divided

1/2 to 3/4 cup half-and-half

5 1/2 cups prepared marinara sauce, drained to remove excess liquid

In a 2-quart saucepan on medium-low heat, heat the olive oil and blend in the flour. Drain the liquid from the shrimp and crab into a bowl, add the liquid to the flour mixture, and stir well. To this sauce, add the cubed cream cheese, salt, crushed garlic, and horseradish and stir until smooth. Add the Asiago cheese and 2 tablespoons Parmesan cheese and stir until smooth.

When the cheese has melted and the sauce is smooth, add the shrimp and crab; blend well. Simmer until heated through. Finally, add the half-and-half a little at a time until the sauce starts to simmer and begins to resemble warm pudding. Let the sauce simmer for 12 to 15 minutes, stirring so it will not scorch on the bottom.

Preheat the oven to 325°F. Spray a shallow 9 x 9-inch baking dish with nonstick spray. Fill the bottom of the dish with the drained marinara sauce and carefully spoon the seafood sauce on top. Sprinkle the rest of the Parmesan cheese on top and bake for 10 to 15 minutes, until heated through. The dip should not brown on top.

YIELD: 4 SERVINGS

Sicilian Scampi

If you enjoy shrimp scampi, you'll like this. Fresh shrimp and a variety of cheeses make a tasty sauce that goes well served over bread or pasta.

2 tablespoons olive oil

½ cup dry white wine

2 tablespoons fresh lemon juice

6 fantail shrimp, uncooked

1 tablespoon finely diced onion

½ teaspoon minced garlic

¼ teaspoon garlic salt

1 tablespoon flour mixed with 1 tablespoon water

½ cup heavy cream

½ cup plus 1 tablespoon finely shredded Asiago cheese

¼ cup finely shredded mozzarella cheese

1 tablespoon finely shredded Romano cheese

4 slices Italian bread, lightly toasted (about 4 to 6 inches long and 1½ inches thick, cut diagonally)

1 green onion, sliced (about 1 tablespoon)

4 black olives, sliced

¼ cup diced tomato

¼ teaspoon crushed red pepper

Heat the olive oil in a saucepan on medium heat and add the wine and lemon juice. When the mixture starts to boil, place the shrimp in the pan and cook until the shrimp curl and they are done. Remove the shrimp but leave the liquid in the pan.

In the same saucepan, add the onion, minced garlic, and garlic salt to the wine mixture and sauté until the onions are transparent. Add the flour-and-water paste, stir, and cook until the sauce is thick. Pour in the cream and stir. Add the Asiago cheese, then the mozzarella cheese, and then the Romano cheese, and whisk constantly after each addition. The sauce should be a medium-thick consistency and smooth. If it's is too thick, add a little water, about ¼ to ⅓ cup, and whisk. Remove the sauce from the heat.

To serve, place the Italian bread on a serving tray in an X shape. Arrange the shrimp between the bread slices. Spoon sauce in the middle of the bread, covering the shrimp. Sprinkle with sliced green onions, olives, and tomatoes. Sprinkle crushed red pepper on top, and more Parmesan cheese.

YIELD: 2 SERVINGS AS AN APPETIZER, OR 1 AS A MAIN DISH

Stuffed Mushrooms

These are easy to make and you can make as many as you want for much less money than you'd spend at a restaurant. These stuffed mushrooms have multiple layers of flavors, with Italian seasonings, clams, and a variety of cheeses.

8 to 12 fresh mushrooms, depending on size

1 (6-ounce) can clams

1 green onion, finely chopped (about 1 tablespoon)

⅛ teaspoon garlic salt

½ teaspoon minced garlic

1 tablespoon butter, melted and cooled

1 teaspoon dried oregano

½ cup Italian-style bread crumbs

1 egg, beaten

2 tablespoons finely shredded Parmesan cheese

1 tablespoon finely shredded Romano cheese

¼ cup plus 2 tablespoons finely shredded mozzarella cheese, divided

¼ cup melted butter

minced parsley, for garnish

Wash the mushrooms, remove the stems, and pat the mushrooms dry. Save the stems for another recipe. Drain the liquid from the clams into a small bowl and set aside. In a mixing bowl, combine the clams, onion, garlic salt, minced garlic, butter, and oregano and blend well. Add the bread crumbs, egg, and the reserved clam juice and blend. Stir in the Parmesan cheese, Romano cheese, and ¼ cup mozzarella cheese and mix well. Place the clam mixture inside the mushroom cavities and slightly mound it.

Preheat the oven to 350°F. Place the mushrooms in a lightly oiled baking dish and pour the butter over the top. Cover the dish with aluminum foil and bake for about 35 to 40 minutes. Remove the cover and sprinkle the remaining 2 tablespoons of freshly grated mozzarella cheese on top and pop the mushrooms back in the oven just so the cheese melts slightly. Garnish with freshly minced parsley.

YIELD: 4 SERVINGS

CopyKat.com's **OLIVE GARDEN®**

Toasted Ravioli

You can easily make this dish at home by using packaged ravioli, and you may wish to consider using more than one variety. Instead of using marinara sauce, you may want to substitute Alfredo sauce.

8 cups vegetable oil

¼ cup water

2 eggs, beaten

1 teaspoon Italian seasoning

1 teaspoon garlic salt

1 cup plain bread crumbs

1 cup flour

1 (16-ounce) package meat-filled ravioli (fresh, or frozen and thawed)

marinara (or Alfredo) sauce

Heat the vegetable oil in a deep-fryer or pot to 350°F. Mix the water with the eggs, beat well, and set aside. Mix the Italian seasoning and garlic salt with the bread crumbs and set this aside. Measure the flour into a bowl and set aside. Working in batches, dip the ravioli in the flour, then in the egg wash, then in the bread crumbs, and carefully place them in the hot oil. Don't fry too many at a time, or the oil won't stay hot enough. Fry the ravioli until golden, remove from the oil, and drain on paper towels. Repeat the process with the remaining ravioli. Serve with your favorite marinara sauce.

YIELD: 8 SERVINGS

CopyKat.com's OUTBACK STEAKHOUSE™

Aussie Cheese Fries

★

These are honestly my favorite thing on the menu at Outback™, and I have a confession to make: I have ordered them as a main dish more than once. Wonderfully simple french fries covered in cheese and topped with crispy bacon—what could be better? Not many things if you are looking for the ultimate french fry fix. Ideally, make the dipping sauce a day ahead so the flavors have plenty of time to blend.

8 cups vegetable oil

1 pound frozen french fries

1 cup shredded Colby Jack cheese (or the cheese labeled as "taco cheese")

6 strips cooked bacon, diced

Heat the oil to 350°F in a large pot (I like to use a Dutch oven). If you do not have a thermometer, you can make sure the oil is hot enough by putting one french fry in: If it cooks immediately, the oil is hot enough; if it sinks to the bottom and the oil barely bubbles, the oil is not ready yet. Fry the french fries in small batches until they are golden brown and float to the top of the oil. Be sure to drain the potatoes on paper towels. Keep the finished fries warm in the oven while the others are cooking. When all the french fries are done and drained, place them on an ovenproof platter. Salt the french fries if you like, and sprinkle on the cheese and cooked bacon. Pop the fries back into the oven until the cheese begins to melt. Serve with Outback Steakhouse Dipping Sauce (page 244).

YIELD: 4 TO 6 SERVINGS

Queso

Pappasito's™ is a chain of Mexican restaurants in Texas, and a favorite menu item is their chips and queso. While I can't give you a recipe for the crispy chips, here's a similar-tasting queso recipe that is simple to prepare.

1½ pounds pasteurized processed cheese	½ cup diced onion
⅓ cup whole milk	¼ teaspoon garlic salt
1 (4-ounce) can green chiles, with liquid	½ cup diced ripe tomatoes, seeds discarded
1 tablespoon minced garlic	

Cut the cheese into 1-inch cubes and place them into a large pot. Over low heat, melt the cheese, add the milk, and stir until blended. Add the chilies with their liquid, garlic, onion, and garlic salt, and stir until the onions are transparent. Remove the sauce from the heat and add the tomatoes before serving.

YIELD: APPROXIMATELY 4 CUPS

Salsa

Fresh vegetables makes this salsa extra special, and if you have a garden, access to a farmers market, or even a wonderful produce department, you won't be buying salsa in a jar anymore.

1 fresh poblano pepper, coarsely chopped

1 fresh jalapeño pepper, stem and seeds removed, finely diced

8 Roma tomatoes

1 small yellow onion, diced (about ⅓ to ½ cup)

½ teaspoon celery salt

⅛ teaspoon dried oregano

¼ cup chopped fresh cilantro

½ teapoon sugar

¼ teaspoon garlic salt

¼ teaspoon black pepper

½ to ¾ cup water

In a moderately hot skillet that has been sprayed with a nonstick spray, brown the coarsely chopped poblano pepper and the jalapeño pepper. Brown and stir the peppers until the skins have turned dark. Add the whole tomatoes and brown them until the skins are dark brown on several sides, then remove the pan from the heat. Add the onion to the hot skillet that has been removed from the heat and stir. In a food processor, combine the celery salt, oregano, cilantro, sugar, garlic salt, and pepper. Pour in the peppers, onions, and tomatoes and add the water a little at a time, just enough so the salsa isn't pasty. Process the salsa just enough so it has a medium consistency—leave it a little chunky. Transfer the salsa back to the hot skillet, then turn up the heat quickly and stir for 3 minutes. Serve hot.

YIELD: 6 TO 8 SERVINGS

Bacon Wrapped Sea Scallops

These have been on the menu at Red Lobster® for a long time because they're so tasty. The scallops are marinated in wine and butter and then wrapped in bacon before cooking.

½ cup (1 stick) butter

1 clove garlic, minced

1 tablespoon lemon juice

½ cup dry white wine

½ teaspoon paprika

½ teaspoon seasoned salt

1½ pounds sea scallops

⅓ pound bacon

In a saucepan, melt the butter, then add the garlic, lemon juice, and wine, plus the paprika and seasoned salt. Remove the pan from the heat, drop the scallops in the pan, and allow them to marinate for about 30 minutes. Preheat the oven to 400°F. Slice the bacon strips in half lengthwise. Wrap each scallop with a half piece of bacon and fasten the bacon with a toothpick. Place the wrapped scallops onto a baking pan and bake for about 8 minutes, then turn them over and cook until they're done, about 8 to 10 minutes more. The scallops are done when they turn white and are firm to the touch.

YIELD: 4 TO 6 SERVINGS

CopyKat.com's

Sugar and Spice Pecans

Walking through an airport, fair, or even some shopping malls, we have all seen the nut vendors. Their nuts are so expensive to purchase, but you can make these quickly and easily at home. You may even want to make a double batch and give some away.

¾ cup sugar

1 teaspoon ground cinnamon

½ teaspoon salt

¼ teaspoon ground nutmeg

¼ teaspoon ground allspice

¼ teaspoon ground cloves

2½ tablespoons water

1 egg white

8 cups pecan halves

Preheat the oven to 275°F. Combine the sugar, cinnamon, salt, nutmeg, allspice, cloves, water, and the egg white in a bowl and mix well. Add the pecans and stir until they are well coated. Spread the pecans in a lightly greased, foil-lined baking sheet. Bake for 50 to 55 minutes, stirring every 10 minutes. Remove the pecans from the pan and allow them to cool on waxed paper. When the nuts have cooled, store them in an airtight container.

YIELD: APPROXIMATELY 8 CUPS

Baked Potato Skins

T.G.I. Friday's® always has delicious appetizers, and hearty baked potato skins are one of my long-standing favorites.

5 medium potatoes	½ cup diced crispy-fried bacon
1 tablespoon melted butter	(about 5 strips)
seasoned salt, to taste	1 green onion, diced
¾ cup shredded cheddar cheese	

Preheat the oven to 350°F. Wash the potatoes well and score them with a fork, 4 or 5 times all around the potato. Bake the potatoes directly on the oven rack until they are fork tender, about 35 minutes. Remove the potatoes from the oven and allow them to cool. Cut the potatoes in half and scoop out the meat of the potato, leaving approximately ¼ inch still on the skin. Turn the oven to 375°F. Brush the potato shells with the melted butter, sprinkle them with the seasoned salt, and bake for 15 to 20 minutes until they are crisp but not dry and hard. Remove the potatoes from the oven and sprinkle them with the cheese, bacon, and onion, them put them back in the oven until the cheese is melted. Serve with sour cream or, for a bit of variety, try Ranch dressing.

YIELD: 4 SERVINGS

Fire Bites

We have all had fried onion rings or fried pickles, but these are fried jalapeño pepper slices. They are no longer available at T.G.I. Friday's®, but you can serve them at home with your favorite queso and you'll have a feast for the spicy-loving folks.

8 cups vegetable oil (enough for your favorite deep-frying system)	2 eggs
2²/₃ cups cracker crumbs	½ cups water
2 cups flour	1 (26-ounce) can sliced jalapeño peppers (not pickled), drained

Heat the oil to 350°F in a deep pan or a deep-fryer. Mix the cracker crumbs and flour together and blend well. In a separate bowl, beat the eggs, add the water, and blend well. Dip the slices of jalapeños in the egg wash, then in the flour and cracker crumb mixture. Dust off any excess dry ingredients, and carefully place the jalapeños in the hot oil. Do not overcrowd the frying pan or deep-fryer. Take care, because the peppers like to pop a little. Fry until golden brown. Remove the jalapeños from the oil with a slotted spoon and drain them on a paper towel. Serve with your favorite queso dip on the side.

YIELD: 8 SERVINGS

Nine-Layer Dip

If there's a required dip to be made for a tailgate event anytime during football season, this is it. This is bean dip brought to a new level, with refried beans, bacon, cheese, taco seasoning, tomatoes, green onions, and so much more. It also makes a great snack or light lunch.

2 strips lean bacon, diced

1 (16-ounce) can refried beans, plain

½ teaspoon taco seasoning

½ cup sour cream

¾ cup shredded cheddar cheese, divided

¾ cup guacamole (frozen or premade is fine)

⅓ cup diced tomatoes (about 1 Roma tomato)

1 tablespoon finely chopped fresh cilantro

2 tablespoons sliced black olives

2 tablespoons finely sliced green onions

In a skillet, fry the diced bacon until it's crispy. Add the refried beans and cook them slowly over low heat, stirring frequently, until the bacon and bacon drippings are mixed through the beans, about 15 minutes. Then remove the pan from the heat. In a separate bowl, mix the taco seasoning with the sour cream.

To build the nine-layer dip, assemble the ingredients in this order on a serving platter:

refried beans spread out, 1 to 1½-inches thick

½ cup cheese

sour cream/taco seasoning mix

guacamole

tomatoes

cilantro

black olives

green onion

¼ cup cheese, for garnish

Serve with crisp corn chips and a very cold beverage of choice.

YIELD: 8 GENEROUS SERVINGS

Buffalo Shrimp

This is a great variation on popcorn shrimp, and it is definitely something a little different. These shrimp make a great party food, or even a light dinner.

3 tablespoons Tabasco sauce

3 tablespoons melted butter

¼ teaspoon freshly ground black pepper

1 (12-ounce) package frozen breaded shrimp

Mix the Tabasco sauce, melted butter, and pepper together. Place the frozen shrimp in an 8 x 8-inch baking dish, pour the Tabasco mixture over the shrimp, and stir well. Cover the dish with plastic wrap and place it in the refrigerator for 1 hour. The shrimp will marinate and absorb all of the sauce.

Preheat the oven to 350°F. Place the shrimp on a flat baking sheet and bake for about 25 minutes. The original Buffalo Shrimp are served with blue cheese dressing, but you can also serve this with Ranch dressing, carrot sticks, and celery sticks on the side.

YIELD: 4 SERVINGS

Salads

✕✕✕✕✕✕✕✕✕✕✕✕✕✕✕✕✕✕✕✕✕✕✕✕

Salads are wonderful, and they can be a light, or even a hearty, meal. Salads can be the nice lettuce variety or they can be filled with pasta, vegetables, or even meat. Included here are several salad recipes that would be perfect to take to a picnic, like the Souper Salad's™ Fettuccine Salad, or Cracker Barrel Old Country Store's® Carrot Salad with Pecans. One thing that I really like about salads is that you can use what you have in your refrigerator to make them, and you don't have to follow any set rules about what to put in—if you have a little extra corn, throw it on. Be experimental, and enjoy yourself in the kitchen.

Krab Salad

Albertsons™ has some of the best imitation crab salads around. Look for bulk imitation crab that is sold at many grocery stores. This salad goes wonderfully as a sandwich filling, on a bed of lettuce, or even in a hulled-out tomato for a light lunch.

2 pounds imitation crab meat

$1/3$ cup diced green onion tops
(the green part only)

$1/2$ cup mayonnaise

Chop the imitation crab meat into small diagonal pieces. Thinly dice the green onion tops (do not use the white part of the onion—its taste is too strong for this salad). Combine the imitation crab, mayonnaise, and green onions together and blend thoroughly. Refrigerate the salad for a couple of hours before serving.

YIELD: 8 SERVINGS

Bacon Ranch Salad ✓

Pasta, mayonnaise, and a few extra ingredients make a nice salad without using a prepackaged mix. Fresh ingredients make it taste wonderfully refreshing. For variation, this is really good with small cubes of cheddar cheese added. You may want to double this recipe.

2 cups dry small shell pasta

3 to 4 peeled baby carrots (or 1 large carrot), shredded

1 (8-ounce) can very young peas, drained (important—young peas are small and crisp)

1 (1-ounce) packet Ranch dressing mix

2 tablespoons Real Bacon Bits

½ teaspoon onion powder

⅔ cup mayonnaise (do not use Miracle Whip)

Bring water to a rolling boil in a saucepan. Add the shell pasta and the shredded carrots and let them boil, uncovered, for 10 minutes. Drain them into a strainer and rinse under cold water.

In a medium-sized bowl, mix together the peas, the entire packet of Ranch dressing mix, bacon bits, onion powder, and mayonnaise. Add the pasta and carrots. Stir until everything is coated with the mayo mixture. Chill and serve.

YIELD: 6 SERVINGS

Carrot Salad with Pecans

Leave it to Cracker Barrel® to reinvent a popular salad. We have all had the delicious carrot and raisin salad before, but adding pecans gives a very nice new take on this classic. For the best results, use pecan halves and chop them into small pieces just before making the salad. Packaged, pre-chopped pecans do not have as good a flavor as they do when you chop them just before you need them.

½ cup chopped pecans

1 (8-ounce) can crushed pineapple, in juice

¼ cup mayonnaise

1 teaspoon sugar

dash of salt

¼ cup raisins

4 cups grated carrots

Place the chopped pecans in a small skillet over medium heat and toast them until they become aromatic. Do not let them burn; there is a fine line between toasted and burnt pecans. Remove the pecans from the skillet and place them on a plate to cool before adding them to the salad. Drain the pineapple and reserve the juice. In a large bowl, combine the mayonnaise, 2 tablespoons reserved pineapple juice, sugar, and salt and whisk well. When the wet ingredients are well mixed, add the raisins, grated carrots, crushed pineapple, and cooled pecans. Use a large spoon to stir the salad together and cover it with plastic wrap. Allow the salad to season by placing it in the refrigerator for a couple of hours before serving.

YIELD: 8 SERVINGS

Fruit Punch Jell-O® Salad ✓

Jell-O® salads are always light and refreshing. Furr's™ makes theirs extra special by adding fruit cocktail, coconut, and miniature marshmallows, so you can turn plain Jell-O® salad into something that can be served even for dessert, if you'd like. This makes a great dish for a potluck.

3 (3-ounce) packages Mixed Fruit Jell-O	1 (14½-ounce) can fruit cocktail, drained
3 cups boiling water	1 cup dried flaked coconut
2½ cups cold water	1 cup miniature marshmallows

Empty the Jell-O packets into a mixing bowl, add the boiling water, and stir to dissolve the Jell-O. Pour the cold water into the Jell-O and blend thoroughly with a whisk. Pour one cup of the Jell-O in a separate small bowl, set it aside, and do not chill it. Place the remaining Jell-O in a 9 x 13-inch pan or another serving dish. Chill the Jell-O in the refrigerator until it is soft-set, about 2 hours.

When the Jell-O is soft-set, remove it from the refrigerator. Place the drained fruit cocktail on top of the Jell-O in an even layer. Sprinkle the coconut on top of the fruit cocktail and evenly arrange the marshmallows on top of everything. Press it all very lightly with the back of a spoon. Finally, pour the reserved liquid Jell-O on top of the marshmallows. Place the dish back into the refrigerator until the salad is completely set.

YIELD: 24 SERVINGS

Lime Jell-O® Salad

Gelatin can be molded and flavored in a million different ways, and the addition of cottage cheese and pecans in this recipe makes for a fine Jell-O® salad. This isn't too sweet, and it's perfect for a meal.

2 (3-ounce) packages Lime Jell-O

2 cups boiling water

1 cup cold water

1 (20-ounce) can crushed pineapple, drained

1 (16-ounce) container small curd cottage cheese

1 (8-ounce) container whipped topping (like Cool Whip)

¼ cup very finely crushed pecans

Empty the Jell-O packets into a mixing bowl, add the boiling water, and stir to dissolve the Jell-O. Pour the cold water into the Jell-O and blend thoroughly with a whisk. To the mixture, add the crushed pineapple, cottage cheese, and whipped topping. Stir until the whipped topping is smooth and blended. There should be no large lumps of topping. Pour the mixture into a 9 x 13-inch pan, sprinkle the pecans on top, and chill until set, about 2 hours.

YIELD: 24 SERVINGS

Coleslaw

So often coleslaw is made without a great deal of variation in the recipe of cabbage, carrots, onions, and the two standard types of dressing, creamy or vinegar-based. This coleslaw, however, is made from chopped cabbage, green onion tops, and a unique dressing that's made with honey mustard, sour cream, and seasonings. If you're looking for a new take on coleslaw, this is the recipe for you. I find this to be a very gentle and fresh-tasting coleslaw that enhances a main course and doesn't overpower it.

DRESSING:
¼ cup mayonnaise
½ cup sour cream
1 tablespoon honey mustard
1½ teaspoons white vinegar
¼ teaspoon salt
½ teaspoon sugar

SALAD:
5 cups chopped cabbage (about ¼-inch pieces; not shredded)
1 cup chopped parsley leaves
¼ cup chopped green onion tops (use just the green part)
¼ teaspoon salt

FOR DRESSING: Blend and stir the mayonnaise, sour cream, honey mustard, and white vinegar together. Add the salt and sugar and stir well. Set the dressing aside.

FOR SALAD: Combine the cabbage, parsley, green onions, and salt in a large bowl.

FOR ASSEMBLY: Mix all the dressing ingredients very well and pour the dressing over the cabbage mixture. Fold in the dressing so everything is coated. This coleslaw can be served immediately or it will keep in the refrigerator for the next day.

YIELD: 8 SERVINGS

Southwest Caesar Salad

Houston's™ makes everything they touch into something special, and their Southwest Caesar Salad is no exception. This recipe combines black beans, corn, and a spicy Caesar dressing along with crispy tortilla chips for a very refreshing meal.

SPICY CAESAR DRESSING:

1 egg yolk

1 tablespoon minced garlic

2 teaspoons Dijon mustard

2 anchovy fillets, minced

1½ teaspoons coarsely ground black pepper

¼ teaspoon salt

½ teaspoon ground coriander

½ teaspoon ground cumin

1 teaspoon Worcestershire sauce

2 teaspoons cold water

½ cup extra-virgin olive oil

½ cup canola oil

1½ tablespoons sambal chili paste (Thai chili paste)

juice of ½ a lemon

juice of ½ a lime

3 tablespoons freshly grated Parmesan cheese

SALAD:

2 heads romaine lettuce, washed and torn into bite-size pieces

1 (16-ounce) can black beans, drained and rinsed with cold water

1 (16-ounce) can corn, drained

½ cup roasted pumpkin seeds

½ cup Cotjia cheese (Mexican white cheese)

julienne-cut multicolored tortilla chips, baked or fried, for garnish

FOR DRESSING: Combine the egg yolk, garlic, mustard, anchovies, pepper, salt, coriander, cumin, Worcestershire sauce, and water in a food processor; process until smooth. With the motor running, pour the olive oil and the canola oil into the egg mixture in a slow, steady stream. When all the oil has been incorporated, add the chili paste, lemon juice, lime juice, and the Parmesan cheese; process until smooth.

FOR SALAD: Spin or pat dry the lettuce and place it in a large salad bowl. Add the 1½ cups of the prepared salad dressing and toss lightly. Add the beans and corn; toss again. Divide the salad among two or four chilled plates, depending on the serving size. Sprinkle with pumpkin seeds and cheese. Garnish with tortilla chips.

∞∞∞

YIELD: 2 LARGE SERVINGS OR 4 APPETIZER SERVINGS

Shredded Carrot Salad

This is a wonderful salad to make any time of the year because you can always find fresh carrots at the store. The combination of carrots, pineapple, and raisins makes for a delightful salad that keeps fresh in the refrigerator so you can make it ahead of time. In many grocery stores, you can purchase carrots that are already shredded, but I recommend that you shred yours just before use for the best flavor.

2 pounds raw carrots, peeled and shredded	1 cup raisins, soaked in water to plump, and drained
1 cup canned chunk pineapple, drained	½ cup powered sugar
1 cup mayonnaise	

In a bowl, combine the carrots, pineapple, mayonnaise, raisins, and powdered sugar; mix well. Chill until ready to serve.

YIELD: 8 SERVINGS

Grilled Chicken Salad

You, too, can make fancy salads at home. This specially marinated grilled chicken salad makes a fantastic light meal.

MARINADE:
2 cups brown sugar

1 cup soy sauce

1 cup sherry

3 cups pineapple juice

½ cup red wine vinegar

1 teaspoon granulated garlic

½ teaspoon ground ginger

SALAD:
7 cups marinade

4 boneless chicken breast

8 cups salad lettuce (2 cups
per serving)

4 hard-cooked eggs
(1 per serving)

8 slices bacon (2 per serving)

32 croutons (about 8 per serving)

12 tomato wedges
(about 3 per serving)

VINAIGRETTE:
1 cup cottonseed oil

1 cup red wine vinegar

¼ clove garlic

1 teaspoon salt

1 teaspoon black pepper

1 teaspoon dried oregano

¼ cup sugar

¼ cup Dijon mustard

FOR MARINADE: In a large bowl, combine the brown sugar, soy sauce, sherry, pineapple juice, vinegar, garlic, and ginger. Mix well. This makes enough marinade for 6 chicken breasts. If you wish to store the marinade, only use enough liquid to cover the chicken in this recipe, and store the rest of the unused marinade in a covered container. The marinade stays fresh for one week.

FOR SALAD: Prepare the marinade and marinate the chicken, for at least 3 hours. Grill the chicken over medium heat for about 5 to 7 minutes on each side. Place the lettuce on a large plate. Slice the chicken and place it on top of the lettuce. Garnish with the egg, bacon, croutons, and tomato wedges.

FOR VINAIGRETTE: Combine the oil, vinegar, garlic, salt, pepper, oregano, sugar, and mustard in a blender; whisk until fully blended. This makes about 2 cups. Add the vinaigrette to the chicken salad or serve it on the side.

∞∞∞∞∞∞∞∞∞∞∞∞∞∞∞∞∞∞∞∞

YIELD: 4 SERVINGS

Fettuccine Salad

Do you love fettuccine Alfredo? If so, you'll enjoy this salad. It features a creamy dressing of Parmesan cheese and freshly cracked pepper, with a touch of garlic. The corn gives the salad a pop of fresh flavor, and this is easy to make for even the novice cook.

8 ounces dry fettuccine	½ teaspoon garlic powder
½ cup frozen corn	1 teaspoon freshly ground pepper
½ cup mayonnaise	salt, to taste
¼ cup grated Parmesan cheese	

Cook and drain the pasta according to the package directions. Mix the pasta and corn in a medium bowl. Mix together the mayonnaise, Parmesan cheese, garlic powder, and pepper in a small bowl. Combine the pasta and sauce, and mix well. Salt to taste. This is best if refrigerated for a couple of hours before serving.

YIELD: 8 SERVINGS

Baja Bean Salad

This is my pick from the Sweet Tomatoes® salad bar restaurant. It's a great, flavorful bean salad. You can make it with common ingredients, and it tastes completely different than ordinary bean salads. This recipe will provide you with a light and healthy side-dish option for your next meal.

SALAD:

1 (15½-ounce) can red beans

1 (15½-ounce) can black beans

1 (15½-ounce) can garbanzo beans

¼ cup diced red onions

⅛ cup chopped fresh cilantro (packed in a cup)

1 tablespoon chopped pickled jalapeño peppers (or a little more if you like)

DRESSING:

¼ cup red wine vinegar

3 tablespoons sugar

¼ teaspoon salt

¼ teaspoon freshly ground pepper

FOR SALAD: Rinse and drain the red beans, black beans, and garbanzo beans. Add the onions, cilantro, and jalapeños.

FOR DRESSING: Combine all the ingredients and mix well.

FOR ASSEMBLY: Pour the dressing over the bean salad and stir well. Cover the salad and let it sit in the refrigerator for a couple of hours to let the flavors blend.

YIELD: 8 SERVINGS

Three Bean Salad

This easy-to-make salad is perfect to take to a potluck or even make a day or two ahead of when you will serve it. If this gets to sit for a bit of time before serving, the flavors will mingle together, making this salad taste oh-so-good.

SALAD:
1 (16-ounce) package frozen green beans

1 (19-ounce) can garbanzo beans

1 (15½-ounce) can dark red kidney beans

½ cup diced green bell pepper

⅓ cup diced yellow onion

½ teaspoon salt

DRESSING:
½ cup red wine vinegar

1 tablespoon sugar

¼ teaspoon freshly ground pepper

¼ teaspoon salt

FOR SALAD: Cook the frozen green beans as directed, but for only 10 minutes. Plunge the green beans into ice water until they're cool and drain the water off. Set the green beans aside to cool. You do not want the green beans to get mushy or overcooked. Rinse and drain the canned garbanzo beans and kidney beans. Pour the garbanzo beans, kidney beans, and green beans into a bowl and add the bell pepper and onion.

FOR DRESSING: Combine the vinegar, sugar, pepper, and salt and mix well.

FOR ASSEMBLY: Pour the dressing on the salad and mix well. The salad should sit in the refrigerator overnight so that the vegetables can marinate. If the dressing seems a little sharp, check the taste after you let the beans marinate. If the salad is still a little too sharp for your taste, add ½ to 1 teaspoon sugar and mix well.

YIELD: 12 SERVINGS

Soups

XXXXXXXXXXXXXXXXXXXXX

Soups are wonderful to make whether you are looking for a light meal or something to warm your soul. I like to make soups to take to work for lunch during the week. They reheat well, and many soups only taste better a couple of days later. With many of these soups, a loaf of garlic bread or even cheesy garlic bread, makes for a great dinner. Here we feature soups in many different cooking styles. My personal favorite is the recipe that tastes like the Olive Garden's® Zuppa Toscana, and I make it often. One thing about making your own soup is you can add extra of your favorite ingredients and make it special just for you.

Broccoli and Cheese Soup

The Black-eyed Pea™ is known for food that tastes home-cooked. You will swear you are back in your grandmother's kitchen when you step into one of their restaurants. This is an incredibly rich and tasty version of their broccoli and cheese soup.

1½ pounds broccoli	¾ teaspoon salt
2 cups (1 pint) half-and-half	pepper, to taste
3 cups water, divided	½ cup cornstarch
1 pound pasteurized processed cheese (like Velveeta)	

Steam the broccoli until it's tender. Place the half-and-half and 2 cups water in the top of a double boiler. Add the cheese, salt, and pepper. Heat the mixture over medium heat until the cheese is melted, then stir in the broccoli. Mix the cornstarch and the remaining 1 cup of water in a small bowl. Stir the cornstarch mixture into the melted cheese and broccoli, and heat the soup in the double boiler until it thickens.

YIELD: 8 SERVINGS

CopyKat.com's **CHILI'S®**

Chicken Enchilada Soup

Chili's® manages to pack in bold flavors without too much heat, and this is one of their signature soups. There are a couple of ingredients that you may have not seen before, like chicken base, which you will find near the bouillon cubes in grocery stores, and masa harina, a type of flour that is used in tortilla making and is sold in the baking aisle.

½ cup vegetable oil

¼ cup chicken base

3 cups diced yellow onions

2 teaspoons ground cumin

2 teaspoons chili powder

2 teaspoons granulated garlic

½ teaspoon cayenne pepper

2 cups masa harina

4 quarts (16 cups) water, divided

2 cups canned crushed tomatoes

½ pound processed American cheese, cut in ½-inch cubes

3 pounds cooked chicken, cut in ½-inch cubes (see note)

In a large pot, combine the oil, chicken base, onions, cumin, chili powder, granulated garlic, and cayenne pepper. Sauté until the onions are soft and clear, about 5 minutes. In a large bowl, combine the masa harina with 1 quart water and stir until all the lumps are gone. If you add the masa harina directly to the soup, it will be difficult to mix in and the soup may be lumpy. Add the masa harina to the pot with the onion mixture and bring everything to a boil. Once the mixture starts to bubble, continue cooking for 2 to 3 minutes, stirring constantly; this will eliminate any raw taste from the masa harina. Add the remaining 3 quarts water. Add the tomatoes and let the soup return to a boil, stirring occasionally. Once the soup is boiling, add the cheese. Cook, stirring occasionally, until the cheese melts. Add the chicken and allow it to heat through.

NOTE: You can substitute uncooked chicken breasts for the cooked cubed chicken. Place the chicken breasts in a medium pot, add enough water to cover, and boil the chicken until it's cooked through, about 30 minutes. The water you cook the chicken breasts in can be used as some of the water you will need in the recipe.

YIELD: 16 TO 20 SERVINGS, 1½ GALLONS

Baked Potato Soup

Baked potato soup is one of the soups that most comforts the soul. A creamy broth filled with potatoes and topped with cheese and bacon is really hard to beat, and this soup is enhanced with fennel.

5 medium russet potatoes

3 cups whole milk

½ cup half-and-half

1¼ teaspoons fennel seeds

½ cup sour cream

1 cup shredded cheddar cheese, divided

1½ teaspoons chives

½ teaspoon salt, or to taste

¼ teaspoon freshly ground pepper, or more to taste

¼ teaspoon celery salt

2½ tablespoons butter

1 green onion, diced

5 strips bacon, diced, fried crispy, and drained

Preheat the oven to 350°F. Wash and scrub the potatoes and pat them dry. Rub the potatoes with butter, place them in a baking pan, and bake for 1 hour and 15 minutes, or until a fork inserted into a potato goes in smoothly. Remove the potatoes from the oven and let them cool slightly.

While the potatoes are cooling, combine the milk, half-and-half, and fennel seeds in a saucepan, and scald the mixture. Scalding is heating milk over a moderate flame just until it reaches the boiling point but is not actually boiling; this will keep the mixture from separating. Then remove the pan from the heat. Let the milk mixture cool slightly, leaving the fennel seeds in.

When the potatoes are cool enough to work with, peel four of them, and then carefully cut them in half and spoon out the cooked potato into a food processor. You should have about 1½ to 2 cups of cooked potato. Leave the skin on the fifth potato, dice it, and set it aside. To the potatoes in the food processor, add the sour cream, chives, salt, pepper, celery salt, and ½ cup plus 1 tablespoon cheddar cheese. Strain the fennel seeds from the warm milk and discard them. Pour the milk mixture into the food processor, and process everything for 1½ to 2 minutes, until smooth. Transfer the mixture into a sauce pan, then add the butter and the reserved diced potato. Stir frequently and simmer over very low heat for about 15 to 20 minutes.

When you're ready to serve, ladle the soup into individual bowls and garnish with the remaining cheddar cheese, bacon, and green diced onion.

◇◇◇◇◇◇◇◇◇◇◇◇◇◇◇◇◇◇◇◇◇◇◇◇◇◇◇

YIELD: 8 SERVINGS

Canadian Cheese Soup

Houston's™ makes different soups every day, so I always find it a challenge to know exactly what they are going to serve. If you make your own soup, you can always have what you want, when you want it. This cheese soup is creamy and rich and goes so well with a piece of crusty garlic bread.

½ cup butter	3 cups half-and-half
1 cup carrots, diced in ⅛-inch cubes	2 pounds pasteurized processed cheese (like Velveeta)
1 cup diced onions	1 tablespoon chopped fresh parsley
½ cup celery, diced in ⅛-inch cubes	diced tomatoes, for garnish
¼ cup flour	diced jalapeños, for garnish
3 cups chicken broth	

Melt the butter in a large, heavy soup pot over medium heat. Add the carrots, onions, and celery all at once. Sauté the vegetables until they're soft, but do not let them brown. Add the flour to the pot and stir to combine. Cook until the mixture begins to turn a light-brown color. Raise the heat to medium-high and add the chicken broth a little at a time. Continue to cook the soup and stir it with a whisk until it thickens to the consistency of a thin pudding. Add the half-and-half and reduce the heat to medium-low; do not let the soup boil. Add the cheese, stirring until it's melted. Just before serving, add the parsley. Garnish with diced tomatoes and jalapeños if desired.

YIELD: 8 SERVINGS

CopyKat.com's **JAMES CONEY ISLAND™**

Chili

James Coney Island™ restaurants are famous in Texas. The next time you're there, don't miss out on your chance to have a taste of what Texans enjoy. The diced meat adds a nice rich flavor to this chili.

2½ pounds chuck steak, tenderized and diced fine

4 tablespoons vegetable oil

2 (10½-ounce) cans beef broth

2 cups water

2 (16-ounce) cans whole tomatoes, with juice

1 tablespoon paprika

5 teaspoons chili powder

1 teaspoon garlic powder

1 teaspoon onion powder

¾ teaspoon seasoned salt

¼ teaspoon garlic salt

¼ teaspoon cayenne pepper

½ teaspoon MSG

5 tablespoons finely ground saltine cracker crumbs

1 to 1¼ cups water (use enough water with dry ingredients to mix into a medium thick, smooth sauce)

In a 4-quart saucepan, lightly brown the diced chuck steak in the vegetable oil, stirring frequently. Add the beef broth and water. Simmer the beef mixture for 1 hour on medium-low heat. While the meat is simmering, purée the tomatoes with their juices in a food processor. Strain the seeds and pulp and measure out 2 cups. After the beef has been simmering for 1 hour, add the tomatoes, paprika, chili powder, garlic powder, onion powder, seasoned salt, garlic salt, cayenne pepper, and MSG to the meat and stir well. Simmer for 45 to 50 minutes on low heat, stirring occasionally.

While the chili is simmering, prepare the thickening agent by combining the saltine cracker crumbs and water. Add enough of the water to make a medium-thick, smooth mixture; you may not use all the water. After the chili has simmered, slowly pour enough of the thickening sauce in to make the chili thick, stirring constantly. You may not need all of the thickener. Simmer on low heat and stir until the chili reaches the desired consistently and is ready to be served.

YIELD: 8 SERVINGS

Zuppa Toscana

★ ▢

Potatoes, Italian sausage, kale, onions, and cream make for a flavorful soup, and this is my personal recipe for Olive Garden's® Zuppa Toscana. While Olive Garden® uses pancetta, it may be difficult to find, and bacon bits make a wonderful substitute with an ingredient you can find easily at your grocery store. You may wish to add about a half-teaspoon of fennel to this for extra flavor.

1 pound Italian sausage links

1 large onion, yellow chopped

2 large russet potatoes sliced in half, then cut in ¼-inch slices

2 (14-ounce) cans chicken broth

1 quart (4 cups) water

2 cloves garlic, minced

⅓ cup Real Bacon Bits (canned are ideal, as they are less fatty than real bacon)

salt and pepper, to taste

2 cups kale or Swiss chard, chopped

1 cup heavy whipping cream

Preheat the oven to 300°F. Bake the sausages for approximately 30 minutes. Drain them on paper towels and cut them into ¼-inch slices.

Place the onion, potatoes, chicken broth, water, and garlic in a large pot, and cook on medium heat until the potatoes are cooked through. Add the sausage, bacon bits, salt, and pepper, and simmer for another 10 minutes. Turn the heat to low and add the kale and whipping cream. Heat through and serve.

◇◇◇◇◇◇◇◇◇◇◇◇◇◇◇◇◇◇◇◇◇◇◇◇◇◇◇

YIELD: 8 SERVINGS

Walkabout® Creamy Onion Soup

★

This wonderfully creamy soup has a flavorful base, then I add tender onions and cheese to make it filling and cheesy.

WHITE SAUCE:
3 tablespoons butter

3 tablespoons flour

1½ cups whole milk

¼ teaspoon salt

SOUP:
2 tablespoons butter

2 cups thinly sliced yellow sweet onions

1 (14-ounce) can chicken broth

2 chicken bouillon cubes

¼ teaspoon salt

¼ teaspoon freshly ground pepper

¼ cup diced pasteurized processed cheese
(like Velveeta cubes, packed in a measuring cup)

1½ to 1 ¾ cup White Sauce
(see recipe below)

shredded cheddar cheese, for garnish

FOR WHITE SAUCE: In a 1-quart saucepan, melt the butter, then add the flour. Cook on medium heat, stirring occasionally, until the flour thickens and comes away from the side of the saucepan. Pour in the milk a little at a time and stir constantly, taking care not to let the mixture get lumpy, then add the salt. The mixture should become like thick pudding. Remove the pan from the heat and set it aside.

FOR SOUP: In a 2-quart saucepan on medium-low heat, melt the butter, then add the onions and cook over low to medium heat, stirring frequently, until the onions are soft and clear but not brown. Add the chicken broth, chicken bouillon cubes, salt, and pepper, and stir until completely heated through. Add the cheese and the White Sauce, which will be thick because it has been removed from the heat. Simmer the soup on medium-low heat, stirring constantly, until the cheese is melted and all the ingredients are blended. Reduce the heat to low and let the soup cook for an additional 30 to 45 minutes. Serve with shredded cheddar cheese as a garnish and some hearty dark bread.

YIELD: 8 SERVINGS

CopyKat.com's **RED LOBSTER®**

Clam Chowder

Enjoying tasty clam chowder just like Red Lobster's® isn't a secret. This soup is brimming with clams, potatoes, and much more. I fill this version with extra flavor by using clam juice, which you can buy in your grocery store. You may want to use a little more in this recipe if you really like the clam flavor.

2 cups peeled, cubed russet potatoes, in ½-inch cubes

½ cup (1 stick) butter

2 tablespoons diced green onion (use only the white bulb)

¼ cup flour

2 cups (16 ounces) half-and-half

1 teaspoon salt, or to taste

2 (6½-ounce) cans minced clams, with juice

⅓ cup bottled clam juice

½ cup whole milk

fresh parsley, minced, for garnish

Place the cubed potatoes in a saucepan, cover them with water, and cook on medium heat until tender. Remove the potatoes from the heat, then drain and set them aside. In a 2-quart saucepan on medium-low heat, melt the butter, then add the green onions and cook until the onions are slightly clear in color. Add the flour and stir briskly. The mixture will start to thicken. Add the half-and-half a little at a time while stirring briskly. The mixture will look like thick cream. Add the salt, the cooked potatoes, the canned clams and their juice, the bottled clam juice, and the milk. On medium-low heat, bring the chowder to a slow boil. Then turn the heat down to low and let the chowder simmer gently for 15 minutes, stirring frequently. Garnish the soup with parsley and serve with hard rolls, freshly whipped butter, and a cozy fire to warm your tummy and your soul.

YIELD: 8 SERVINGS

Chili

Steak 'n Shake's™ chili is one of my favorite recipes. Unlike many types of chili that use regular ground meat, this one uses chuck roast. My suggestion is to buy a chuck roast, trim off the excess fat, and grind the meat yourself. If you are unable to do that, many grocery stores sell a coarse grind of meat often labeled as "ground for chili," and this works well, too.

2 pounds lean, coarsely ground beef chuck

1½ cups diced onion

1 teaspoon celery salt

4 (8-ounce) cans tomato sauce

2 (16-ounce) cans light kidney beans, with liquid

2 teaspoons garlic powder

1½ teaspoons garlic salt

2 tablespoons plus 1 teaspoon chili powder

1 cup water

½ teaspoon salt

½ teaspoon pepper

2 (8-ounce) cans tomato paste

In a skillet on medium-low heat, sauté the ground beef and onions. When the beef is cooked, drain all the grease and transfer the mixture to a medium-large sauce pan. Add the celery salt, tomato sauce, kidney beans, garlic powder, garlic salt, chili powder, water, salt, and pepper, and stir to combine. Cover the pan and let the chili simmer on low heat for 1 hour, stirring frequently. After the chili has been cooking for an hour, add the tomato paste and stir well. Cover the pan and let the chili simmer for an additional 30 minutes.

YIELD: 10 SERVINGS

CopyKat.com's STEAK 'N SHAKE™

Five Way Chili ✓

★ ▯

So once you have your Steak 'n Shake™ Chili (page 86), you can eat it as its own dish like you normally would, or you can enjoy the restaurant's most popular way of serving it: this Five Way Chili. Personally, I order this dish every time I go there.

1 recipe Steak 'n Shake® Chili (page 86)

1 pound dry spaghetti

¾ cup chili sauce (like Heinz; see note)

12 ounces shredded Colby Jack cheese

1 medium onion, diced

Prepare the Steak 'n Shake Chili according to the recipe directions. Prepare the spaghetti as directed on the package and drain the water off. To assemble each serving, place a generous helping of spaghetti in a shallow bowl or plate and add ¾ cup Steak 'n Shake Chili, 2 tablespoons chili sauce, ½ cup cheese, and diced onions, to taste. Any leftover chili can be combined with crisp tortilla chips for a light lunch or a great snack.

NOTE: Chili sauce can be purchased at most grocery stores in the condiment area. It is sold in a glass bottle, and looks somewhat like the old glass Heinz ketchup bottles.

YIELD: 6 SERVINGS

Broccoli and Cheese Soup

This version of broccoli and cheese soup is lighter than the traditional one that's made with heavy cream. It has fresh broccoli, and I use low-fat milk to help make it diet-friendly. This soup is best eaten when it's freshly made. Be sure to serve it with some crusty bread for a filling meal.

4 cups fresh broccoli florets	¾ teaspoon celery salt
3-inches broccoli stalks, diced	¼ teaspoon seasoned salt
⅓ cup diced yellow onion	½ teaspoon sugar
4 cups water	2 cups low-fat milk

In a large pot, cover the broccoli florets, broccoli stalks, and onions with the water and simmer until the broccoli and onions are tender. Remove ¾ cup of the broccoli florets and set aside. Cook the remaining broccoli and onions until soft. Remove from the heat and strain the broccoli and onions.

In a blender, combine the broccoli and onions, celery salt, seasoned salt, sugar, and milk. Blend until smooth. Pour the mixture into a saucepan, add the reserved broccoli florets, and let the soup simmer on medium-low heat for 20 to 25 minutes.

YIELD: 6 SERVINGS

Clam Chowder

Sweet Tomatoes® is a great salad bar—they feature salads, soups, pastas, and more, and everything is made fresh daily. This version of clam chowder features a nice rosemary flavor that is unexpected but really enhances the soup.

3 medium Idaho potatoes

2 cups whole milk, divided

½ cup half-and-half

3 slices lean bacon, diced

½ cup diced yellow onion

1 (6½-ounce) can minced clams, with juice

¼ teaspoon dried thyme

¼ teaspoon finely minced fresh rosemary

½ teaspoon celery salt

¼ teaspoon sugar

2 tablespoons flour (optional)

Wash and peel the potatoes and place them in a medium-sized pot. Cover the potatoes with water, bring the water to a boil, and cook for 20 to 25 minutes. When the potatoes have cooled slightly, slice them julienne style. You should have about 2 cups sliced potatoes.

Combine 1½ cups milk and the half-and-half in a saucepan on medium heat. Scald the mixture by heating it just until it starts to boil, then immediately remove the pan from the stove and set it aside. Scalding milk will help prevent it from curdling.

In a large pan, fry the bacon on medium-high heat to render the grease. When the bacon is done, carefully take it from the pan and leave the grease. Add the onions to the bacon drippings and sauté until they're clear. Add the scalded milk, cooked potatoes, clams with their juice, thyme, rosemary, celery salt, and sugar. Bring the soup to a slow simmer and cook for 25 to 30 minutes, stirring occasionally. If you like your chowder thicker, at this point it can be thickened by adding 2 tablespoons flour to the remaining ½ cup milk, mixing well, then slowly adding the milk to the chowder, stirring constantly, until it is as thick and creamy as desired.

YIELD: 6 SERVINGS

Tomato and Onion Soup

This is a low-fat, vegetarian soup. This soup tastes fresh, with thinly sliced onions, Roma tomatoes, and fresh herbs, and you can prepare it in no time. To keep the fresh taste, do not store the soup for too long.

2½ cups thinly sliced yellow onions

¼ cup olive oil

4 cups tomato juice

2 cups water

1½ teaspoons celery salt

1½ tablespoons minced fresh basil

3 teaspoons minced fresh oregano

2½ cups diced fresh Roma tomatoes

croutons

In a large soup pot on medium heat, sauté the onions in the olive oil until they turn transparent but not brown. When the onions are transparent, add the tomato juice, water, celery salt, basil, and oregano. Cook the soup, stirring occasionally, for 20 to 25 minutes on medium heat. Add the fresh tomatoes and simmer for 15 to 20 minutes longer. Serve with croutons on top.

YIELD: 8 SERVINGS

French Onion Soup

French onion soup isn't as difficult to make as you might think. The key is carefully caramelizing the onions to get their special flavor. The dry white wine is a wonderful addition, but it can be omitted if you like.

1 tablespoon olive oil	1 tablespoon flour
6 tablespoons butter, divided	8 cups beef broth
3 pounds medium yellow onions, thinly sliced	2 cups dry white wine
1 teaspoon sugar	salt and black pepper, to taste
2 teaspoons salt	4 hamburger buns
	8 slices provolone cheese

Over medium heat, combine the olive oil and 3 tablespoons of the butter in a large, heavy stock pot. Add the sliced onions, then cover and cook, stirring occasionally, until the onions are soft and translucent. Increase the heat to high, remove the lid, and add the sugar and salt. Sauté, stirring often, until the onions are very soft and a deep golden brown color.

Reduce the heat to medium, sprinkle in the flour, and cook, stirring constantly, for 2 to 3 minutes. Add about 2 cups of the beef broth and stir to blend, then add the remaining beef broth and the wine. Season to taste with salt and pepper, and simmer for 30 minutes.

Preheat the oven to 425°F. Brush the cut side of the hamburger buns with the remaining butter and place them buttered side up in the oven to brown. When the buns have browned, remove them from the oven. To serve, gather eight small ovenproof bowls and spoon in the soup. Fill the bowls with soup and add one bun-half per bowl, toasted side up. Add one slice of provolone on top of each bowl, place the bowls in a baking dish, and put the dish into the oven. When the cheese has toasted, remove the pan.

Instead of hamburger buns, you may wish to use baguette slices. Also, you do not need to toast the cheese in the oven. You can simply top the soup with unmelted cheese and serve.

YIELD: 8 SERVINGS

Chili

Wendy's® makes this classic recipe fresh every day, and you can do the same. Tomato juice really enhances the flavor of this chili, as does the chili powder, though you may want to start off with a little less chili powder. I find that ¼ cup isn't too hot, but is very flavorful.

2 pounds freshly ground beef

4 cups (1 quart) tomato juice

1 (29-ounce) can tomato purée

1 (15-ounce) can red kidney beans, drained

1 medium onion, chopped (about 1½ cups)

½ cup celery, diced

¼ cup green bell pepper, diced

¼ cup chili powder (you may want to use less)

1 teaspoon cumin (if you like real flavor, add more)

1½ teaspoons garlic powder

1 teaspoon salt

½ teaspoon black pepper

½ teaspoon dried oregano

½ teaspoon sugar

⅛ teaspoon cayenne pepper

In a frying pan, brown the ground beef, then drain off the fat. Put the beef and the remaining ingredients into a 6-quart pot. Cover the pot and let the chili simmer for 1 to 1½ hours, stirring every 15 minutes.

YIELD: 12 SERVINGS

Main Dishes

The entrée is the centerpiece of a meal, and meals are often planned around it. Gathered here is a wide selection of main dishes, including pasta, beef, and poultry recipes, and even some that are vegetarian. Included are some dishes that are easy to prepare—you could have them done faster than you could go out and pick something up. In many of the pasta dishes, you will have the sauce or other topping done at the same time the pasta is finished cooking. It's so easy, there's no need to go out.

Some of the recipes are home-style favorites, like a meatloaf that tastes just like Boston Market's®. If you have never tried barbecue-style shrimp, I would highly recommend the recipe that tastes just like Bubba Gump's™. There are enough different recipes that you and your loved ones will enjoy new and different meals for many nights.

CopyKat.com's **ARMSTRONG'S™**

Turkey Devonshire

Several years ago I spent about a month in Pittsburgh, Pennsylvania. Armstrong's™ quickly became my favorite restaurant there, and I had never had a Turkey Devonshire sandwich before. It's made of juicy turkey meat, fresh ripe tomatoes, and sourdough bread, all topped with a rich cheese sauce.

1 cup Armstrong's Cheese Sauce (page 230)	¼ pound cooked deli-style turkey
2 slices sourdough bread, slightly toasted	2 large slices tomato
	dash of paprika

Preheat the oven to 350°F. Prepare the cheese sauce according to the recipe directions. Place toasted slices of bread on an ovenproof plate or a pie dish. Place the meat and then the tomato slices on top of the bread. Pour the cheese sauce over everything and sprinkle the top with some paprika. Bake for about 10 minutes, until the cheese sauce browns.

YIELD: 1 SANDWICH

Buffalo Chicken Sandwich

Since there aren't too many Bennigan's™ around now, you may need to make your own buffalo chicken sandwich. Our recipe tastes just like the real thing.

8 cups vegetable oil, for deep-frying	1 hamburger bun
½ cup flour	2 tablespoons hot sauce
½ teaspoon salt	1 leaf green leaf lettuce
1 boneless, skinless chicken breast	2 slices tomato
½ cup milk	1 red onion, sliced (if it's strong, only use a few rings)
	blue cheese dressing

In a large pot or a deep-fryer, heat the oil, just enough to cover the chicken, to 350°F. In a shallow dish, combine the flour and salt and mix well. Completely cover the chicken breast in plastic wrap and gently pound it with a flat object, such as a frying pan, until it is flat and even. Dip the chicken in the milk and then in the seasoned flour. Dip it in the milk again, and then the seasoned flour again. Refrigerate the battered chicken for 10 to 15 minutes. Fry the chicken in the oil for 10 minutes, or until golden brown. Drain on paper towels. Toast or grill the face of the bun. When the chicken breast is drained, transfer it to a plastic bowl with a lid. Pour the hot sauce in the bowl, put the lid on, and shake it gently to coat the chicken with the sauce. Put the chicken on the toasted bun and top it with lettuce, tomato, and onion. Serve the sandwich open-face, with blue cheese dressing on the side.

YIELD: 1 SANDWICH

Monte Cristo Sandwich

OK, so this sandwich is decadent. Here we stack a triple-deck sandwich filled with turkey, ham, and two types of cheese, then we dip it into an egg batter and fry it until it is golden brown. Serve this sandwich with raspberry preserves, a pickle garnish, and your favorite french fries.

SANDWICH:

3 slices cooked deli-style turkey

3 slices Swiss cheese

3 slices wheat bread

3 slices cooked deli-style ham

3 slices American cheese

8 cups vegetable oil, for deep-frying

powdered sugar

BATTER:

1 egg

1 to 1¼ cups water

½ teaspoon salt

1 teaspoon sugar

1½ cups flour

1 tablespoon baking powder

FOR SANDWICH: Place the turkey and Swiss cheese on one slice of bread and the ham and American cheese on another slice of bread. Place a third slice of bread in-between the meats and secure the corners of the triple-decker sandwich with toothpicks.

FOR BATTER: Place the egg in a mixing bowl, add the water, and beat together. Add the salt, sugar, flour, and baking powder. Beat the batter until smooth.

FOR ASSEMBLY: In a large skillet or deep-fryer, heat the oil to 350°F. Dip the sandwich in the batter and carefully cover all the sides. Carefully place the sandwich in the hot oil and fry until golden. When the sandwich has turned a warm gold color, remove it from the hot oil and place it on a paper towel. Let the sandwich cool for a few minutes before removing the toothpicks. Before serving, slice the sandwich into fourths and sprinkle it with powdered sugar.

YIELD: 1 SANDWICH

CopyKat.com's **BOSTON MARKET®**

Meatloaf ✓

Home-style meatloaf is a favorite food that so many of us long for. Eating it brings back wonderful memories of days gone by. It is hard to beat a meatloaf that tastes like Boston Market's®. They use high-quality ground chuck and season it well with onions, tomatoes, garlic, and more. This meatloaf is glazed with a wonderful sweet tomato sauce.

MEATLOAF:
1½ pounds lean ground beef chuck

½ cup minced onions

½ teaspoon garlic salt

¾ cup diced tomatoes, drained

¾ cup plain bread crumbs

1 egg

TOPPING:
¾ cup tomato sauce

2 tablespoons sugar

FOR MEAT MIXTURE: Preheat the oven to 350°F. Mix the ground beef, onions, garlic salt, tomatoes, bread crumbs, and the egg until well blended. Place the mixture in a lightly greased 8 x 4-inch bread pan and bake at for 45 minutes. Remove the loaf from the oven and drain any excess grease from the pan.

FOR TOPPING: Mix the tomato sauce and sugar together.

FOR ASSEMBLY: Pour the topping over the meatloaf and put it back in the oven to finish baking, about 30 minutes, depending on the oven; check for doneness by using a knife to be sure the meat is cooked.

YIELD: 8 SLICES

Cajun Shrimp

Life might be like a box of chocolates, but no one makes shrimp like Bubba Gump™ does—in my opinion, this is the only place for it. Now, if you have never had this, barbecue shrimp isn't cooked on a grill— it's prepared on your stove. The shrimp cooks in a tangy, buttery sauce that has a touch of spice to it.

½ cup butter

1 tablespoon oregano

2 tablespoons chopped garlic

1 tablespoon cayenne pepper

1 pound large shrimp (31/35 count), tail on

fresh lemon juice

In a large skillet, combine the butter, oregano, garlic, and cayenne pepper. Cook on medium-high heat so the garlic begins to smell aromatic. Stir well to combine the seasonings into the butter. Add in the shrimp, stirring occasionally, until the shrimp are pink, about 5 to 7 minutes. Serve with plenty of garlic bread so you can savor all of the sauce. Don't forget to squeeze a little fresh lemon juice on top!

YIELD: 2 SERVINGS

CopyKat.com's **CAJUN CAFÉ™**

Bourbon Chicken

Cajun food is wonderfully spicy without being too hot. Bourbon chicken is served in many shopping malls and is a great way to use less-expensive cuts of chicken. You can use chicken breast for this, but I really like the dark meat. These small, tender pieces of chicken are covered in a sweet and spicy Cajun-style sauce.

4 tablespoons soy sauce

½ cup brown sugar

½ teaspoon garlic powder

1 teaspoon powdered ginger

2 tablespoons dried minced onion

½ cup Jim Beam Bourbon Whiskey

1 pound chicken leg or thigh meat, cut in bite-size chunks

2 tablespoons white wine, like a Chardonnay

Start the night before. In a large bowl, mix the soy sauce, brown sugar, garlic powder, powdered ginger, dried onion, and bourbon. Pour the marinade over the chicken pieces in a bowl. Cover and refrigerate the chicken, stirring often, for several hours (overnight is best).

Preheat the oven to 350°F, and bake the marinated chicken for 1 hour in a single layer, basting every 10 minutes with the marinade. Remove the chicken from the oven and scrape the pan juices with all the brown bits into a frying pan. Heat the juices and add the white wine. Stir and add the chicken. Cook together for 1 minute and serve.

YIELD: 4 SERVINGS

Chicken Madeira

★ 🪑

After I ate this Chicken Madeira, I was on a mission to re-create this recipe. Madeira, a sweet, savory wine, really makes this dish, especially when you combine it with beef broth. The chicken is lightly browned, then you make a creamy wine sauce and top the dish with asparagus and mozzarella cheese. Serve this with a side of pasta for a hearty meal.

4 boneless, skinless chicken breasts	3 cups Madeira wine
salt and pepper, to taste	2 cups beef broth
6 tablespoons butter, divided	¼ teaspoon ground black pepper
1 tablespoon olive oil	8 asparagus spears
2 cups sliced fresh mushrooms	4 slices mozzarella cheese

Pound the chicken breasts flat by covering each breast with plastic wrap and using a mallet to flatten the chicken to approximately ¼-inch thick. Season each side of the breasts with salt and pepper.

In a large skillet, heat together 2 tablespoons of the butter and the olive oil over medium heat; do not let the butter brown. Sauté the chicken breasts until the chicken has browned a little, about 4 to 6 minutes on each side. Remove the chicken breasts, place them on a plate, and cover with foil.

Turn the heat to medium and add 2 more tablespoons of butter to the skillet that the chicken has been cooked in. Add the mushrooms and sauté for a few minutes. Add the Madeira wine, beef broth, the remaining butter, and pepper and bring the sauce to a boil. Allow the sauce to boil for 2 minutes before reducing the heat, then let it simmer for about 20 minutes, or until the sauce has reduced to about half of the original volume. The sauce will thicken and turn a dark brown color when it is done.

Fill a medium saucepan halfway up with water and bring it to a boil. Season the water with salt and toss in the asparagus. Keep an eye on this step—you don't want to overcook your asparagus. Depending on the thickness of the spears, this could take up to 3 to 5 minutes. When it's finished, drop the asparagus in a bowl of ice water to stop the cooking. The asparagus should be slightly tender when done, but not mushy.

Set the oven to broil. Arrange the cooked chicken breasts on a baking pan and cross 2 asparagus spears over each fillet. Top each one with a slice of mozzarella cheese and broil for 3 to 4 minutes or until the cheese begins to slightly brown.

Serve by arranging 2 chicken breast fillets on each plate and spooning 3 to 4 tablespoons of the Madeira sauce over the chicken.

YIELD: 2 LARGE SERVINGS

Crusted Chicken Romano

Not only do they make fantastic cheesecake, The Cheesecake Factory® also has delicious Romano chicken. If you like Olive Garden's® Parmesan-Crusted Chicken (page 124), you'll like this recipe, as they are very similar. I would suggest that you serve this with pasta and either a meat sauce or even an Alfredo sauce.

2 boneless, skinless chicken breasts	½ teaspoon salt
	¼ teaspoon pepper
1 egg, beaten	2 tablespoons shredded Romano cheese
2 teaspoons water	
½ cup flour	2 tablespoons vegetable oil

Pound the chicken breasts flat by covering each breast with plastic wrap and using a mallet to flatten the chicken to approximately ½-inch thick. Whisk together the egg and the water. In a separate shallow dish, combine the flour, salt, and pepper and mix to combine the seasonings throughout the flour. Dip the flattened chicken breasts into the flour mixture, then the egg mixture, and cover each one with shredded Romano cheese. Heat the oil in a frying pan on medium-high heat and cook the chicken in the pan until golden brown, about 5 to 7 minutes on each side.

YIELD: 2 SERVINGS

Margarita Grilled Chicken

Often I go home after working all day and wonder what I can make for dinner. My first impulse is to pull chicken breasts out of the freezer and create something. Here, all you need is some margarita mix to help give the chicken a citrus flavor. These are really easy to make, and they taste fantastic the next day on top of a salad.

4 boneless, skinless chicken breasts	black beans
1 cup liquid margarita mix	Mexican rice
freshly ground black pepper, to taste	pico de gallo

Pour the margarita mix over the chicken breasts and let them marinate for 2 hours in the refrigerator. After they've marinated, drain the margarita mix and dust the chicken with black pepper. Either cook the chicken on a grill, or if you don't have a grill, spray an iron skillet with nonstick spray and bring the pan to medium-high temperature, then cook the chicken breasts until they're done, about 5 to 7 minutes on each side. Serve the chicken breasts on top of black beans and with your favorite Mexican rice and a generous helping of pico de gallo.

YIELD: 4 SERVINGS

Monterey Chicken

Chicken breasts have become a staple of dinners at home because you can turn them into just about anything. Chili's® take on the ordinary chicken breast will have your mouth watering. A grilled chicken breast is covered with bacon slices, tangy barbecue sauce, and topped off with melted cheese.

4 boneless, skinless
chicken breasts

salt and pepper, to taste

8 teaspoons barbecue sauce

8 slices very crispy bacon

1 cup mixture of shredded
Monterey jack and sharp
cheddar cheese

½ cup chopped tomatoes

¼ cup sliced chives

Pound the chicken breasts flat by covering each one with plastic wrap and using a mallet to flatten it somewhat; season with salt and pepper. Spray a skillet with nonstick spray and cook the chicken over medium heat for about 5 to 7 minutes on each side until browned. Transfer to a serving plate. Top each chicken breast with 2 teaspoons of barbecue sauce, 2 slices of bacon, and cheese. To melt the cheese, broil the chicken breasts in the oven or microwave them for about 1 minute on high heat. Sprinkle with a small amount of cold chopped tomatoes and chives.

YIELD: 4 SERVINGS

Chicken Casserole ✓

Do you enjoy home-style casseroles? If so, you'll love this one. I personally love these types of dishes because I can make them ahead of time and reheat them later. Many of us struggle to put dinner on the table in the evening with everything else we have to do. This casserole is simple to make, and you can use leftover chicken, or even canned chicken, if you are in a bind. A crunchy cornbread topping sits on warm chicken and a creamy sauce.

CORNBREAD TOPPING:
1 cup yellow cornmeal

⅓ cup flour

1½ teaspoons baking powder

½ teaspoon baking soda

1 tablespoon sugar

½ teaspoon salt

2 tablespoons vegetable oil

¾ cup buttermilk

1 egg

½ cup butter, melted

CHICKEN FILLING:
2 tablespoons butter

¼ cup chopped yellow onion

½ cup thinly sliced celery

1¾ cups chicken broth

1 (10-ounce) can cream of chicken soup

1 teaspoon salt

¼ teaspoon freshly ground pepper

2½ cups cooked chicken breast, cut into bite-size pieces

FOR CORNBREAD TOPPING: Preheat the oven to 375°F. Mix the cornmeal, flour, baking powder, baking soda, sugar, salt, oil, buttermilk, and the egg together in a mixing bowl until smooth. Pour the batter into a greased 8 x 8-inch baking pan and bake for 20 to 25 minutes; you know it's done when you gently shake the casserole and it doesn't wiggle. Remove the cornbread from the oven and let it cool completely. When it's cool, crumble the cornbread and place 3 cups of cornbread crumbs in a mixing bowl. Add the melted butter to the crumbs and mix well. Set aside.

FOR CHICKEN FILLING: Preheat the oven to 350°F. In a saucepan on medium-low heat, melt the butter and sauté the onions and celery until transparent, stirring occasionally. Add the chicken broth, cream of chicken soup, salt, and pepper. Stir until well blended and the cream of chicken soup is dissolved completely. Add the chicken and stir until the mixture reaches a low simmer. Let simmer for 5 minutes, then remove the pan from the heat. Transfer the chicken filling to a buttered 2½-quart casserole dish or four individual casserole dishes.

FOR ASSEMBLY: Spoon the cornbread topping on top of the chicken; do not stir it into the chicken filling. Bake for 35 to 40 minutes. The crumbs will turn a golden yellow. Serve with a side of country green beans or a salad for a hearty meal.

◇◇◇◇◇◇◇◇◇◇◇◇◇◇◇◇◇◇◇◇◇◇◇◇◇

YIELD: 8 SERVINGS

CopyKat.com's **CRACKER BARREL OLD COUNTRY STORE®**

Chicken Tenders

★

We all loved the family favorites we had when we were growing up, and who captures them better than Cracker Barrel®? This recipe gives you the restaurant taste without having to leave home. You can pick up chicken tenderloins at the grocery store, or even at most warehouse clubs, and with a couple of extra ingredients you will have a tasty dinner.

½ cup Italian salad dressing, spices drained and discarded

1 teaspoon fresh lime juice

1½ teaspoons honey

1 pound chicken breast tenders

Mix the Italian dressing, lime juice, and honey together. Pour the mixture over the chicken tenders, making sure all the tenders are covered, and let them marinate for 1 hour. Sauté the tenders in a nonstick pan or grill until they're light golden in color but aren't dry.

YIELD: 4 SERVINGS

CopyKat.com's DENNY'S®

Bacon Caesar Burger

🍽️ ⏱️

I loved when Denny's® served this burger in their restaurants, but now it's discontinued. This burger's creamy Caesar dressing, bacon, red onion, and ripe tomatoes make it irresistible.

1 hamburger bun	2 slices tomato
1 hamburger patty	2 slices Monterey Jack cheese
1 leaf romaine lettuce	2 slices bacon, cooked
2 hamburger-sliced dill pickles	¼ cup Caesar salad dressing, served on the side
1 slice red onion	

Cook the hamburger patty for about 5 minutes on each side, seasoning with salt and pepper. If you like your burger a little more on the rare side, it will take less time. Toast the bun separately. I always put a little butter on each side of the bun and toast it slightly in a skillet, but you can even do this in the oven using the broiler. Assemble your burger like this (starting from the bottom bun):

bottom bun
lettuce
tomatoes
pickles
onion
hamburger patty
Monterey Jack cheese
bacon, placed crossways
top bun

YIELD: 1 SERVING

CopyKat.com's **HOOTERS™**

Hot Wings

Unlike many other restaurants that serve hot wings, Hooters™ batters their wings before frying them, so you have crunchy, crispy wings bathed in hot sauce. These wings are perfect for a tailgating party or anytime you have a large gathering—but you'll have to provide your own Hooters™ girls.

2 cups whole-wheat flour	¼ teaspoon cayenne pepper
1 cup all-purpose flour	4½ to 5 pounds chicken wings
2½ teaspoons salt	Hooters' Hot Wing Sauce
1 teaspoon paprika	(page 235)

In a large mixing bowl, mix the whole-wheat flour, all-purpose flour, salt, paprika, and cayenne pepper together, and blend well. Cut the chicken wings into drumettes and flappers. Wash and drain the chicken. Coat the chicken in the flour mixture and refrigerate the wings for 90 minutes. Prepare the Hooters Hot Wing Sauce. When you're ready to deep-fry the chicken wings, heat the oil to 375°F in a large pot or deep-fryer. Place the chicken pieces into the hot oil and do not crowd them. Fry the wings until they're golden brown, then remove them from the oil and drain them on paper towels. When all the wings have been fried, place them in a large bowl. Add the Hooters' Hot Wing Sauce and mix completely. Use a fork or tongs to place the chicken pieces on a serving platter. Serve immediately (and with lots of paper towels!).

YIELD: 12 SERVINGS

Mini Buffalo Chicken Sandwiches

Jack in the Box® makes some wonderful mini sirloin burgers, but they also serve up mini buffalo chicken sandwiches. These are easy to make and are perfect for a party, a tailgate celebration, or even any night for dinner. Be sure to use Frank's® RedHot® Sauce to make these sandwiches spicy. Frank's® is what Jack in the Box® uses, and it is one of the best hot sauces around.

1 (13-ounce) package chicken nuggets	buttermilk Ranch salad dressing
1 (12-count) package heat-and-serve rolls	Frank's RedHot Sauce
	iceberg lettuce

Prepare the chicken nuggets as directed on the package. Cook the heat-and-serve rolls as directed on the package. Split open the rolls. Coat the bottom bun with buttermilk Ranch dressing, and then add one chicken nugget per roll. Add about 1 teaspoon of Frank's RedHot sauce to the top of the chicken nugget and then top with iceberg lettuce and the top bun.

YIELD: 12 SANDWICHES

Mini Sirloin Burgers

These burgers are simple to make and would be great at a tailgate party, a sleepover, or for an evening of staying in watching movies. We use heat-and-serve rolls for the buns here because this is a small roll most people have access to, but if your store or local bakery makes a different type of roll, you may want to use those. These burgers are made with ground sirloin, American cheese, a tangy pickle, sweet ketchup, and grilled onions. We imagine you'll find these tasty.

1 (12-count) package heat-and-serve rolls

1 pound ground sirloin

½ teaspoon seasoned salt

1 teaspoon black pepper

½ an onion

1 tablespoon peanut oil

6 to 8 slices American cheese

6 to 8 pickle slices

ketchup

Cook the heat-and-serve rolls according to the package directions. Combine the ground sirloin, seasoned salt, and pepper. Mix well. Slice the onion thinly and add it to a skillet with the peanut oil. Cook the onions slowly and do not brown them. When the onions are almost translucent, make 6 to 8 ½-inch thick hamburger patties from the ground sirloin, and place them in the hot pan with the onions. Grill the hamburgers for 4 to 5 minutes before turning them. Flip the hamburgers and remove the onions. When the hamburger patties are done, assemble the mini burgers like this: bottom bun, pickles, hamburger patty, 1 slice of cheese, grilled onions, ketchup, top bun. Serve quickly.

YIELD: 6 TO 8 SANDWICHES

Coconut Shrimp

Coconut shrimp is different than most fried shrimp. Sure, they're all fried, but there is more to love in coconut shrimp. The shrimp is butterflied, coated with a batter, and then rolled in coconut. When fried, the coconut gives the shrimp a very sweet and nutty flavor.

8 cups vegetable oil, for deep-frying	1 tablespoon sugar
2 eggs	1 teaspoon salt
¼ cup water	½ cup flour
⅔ cup cornstarch, divided	1 pound medium-large fresh shrimp, cleaned, shelled, and butterflied
1 (7-ounce) package premium flaked coconut (small flake, if possible; see note)	

In a large pot or deep-fryer, heat the oil to 350°F. In a small bowl, mix the eggs and water. Set aside. Place ⅓ cup cornstarch in a bowl. In a separate bowl, mix the remaining ⅓ cup cornstarch with the coconut, sugar, salt, and flour and blend well. Heat oil for deep-frying. Roll the shrimp in the plain cornstarch, then in the egg wash, and then finally roll them in the coconut mixture. Place the shrimp in the hot oil and deep-fry until done. The shrimp will float to the top when cooked; take care not to overcook them. Serve with Joe's Crab Shack's Pineapple Dipping Sauce (page 239). Yum-yum.

NOTE: We have found the results to be slightly better when you process the coconut in a blender for a few seconds. It will grate up the coconut just a bit more.

◊◊◊◊◊◊◊◊◊◊◊◊◊◊◊◊◊◊◊◊◊◊◊◊◊◊

YIELD: 4 SERVINGS

CopyKat.com's JOE'S CRAB SHACK™

Popcorn Shrimp

So often popcorn shrimp can be a little dull, and it seems like they hide the shrimp in puffs of fried breading. Here we add a secret ingredient (well, not so secret) to the batter—brown sugar. The brown sugar enhances the batter and helps it become nice and golden before the smaller shrimp become overdone.

1 pound small fresh shrimp, cleaned and shelled

1 teaspoon garlic powder

1 teaspoon brown sugar

1½ teaspoons Tabasco sauce

2 eggs

¼ cup water

⅓ cup flour

1 cup saltine cracker meal

⅓ cup plain bread crumbs

½ teaspoon paprika

1 teaspoon Creole seasoning

4 tablespoons cornstarch

8 cups vegetable oil, for deep-frying

Place the shrimp in a bowl and add the garlic powder, brown sugar, and Tabasco sauce and mix well. Marinate the shrimp for 30 minutes in the refrigerator.

While the shrimp is marinating, beat the eggs with the water, blend well, and set aside. In a separate bowl, mix the flour, cracker meal, bread crumbs, paprika, and Creole seasoning together and blend well. Put the cornstarch in its own bowl. Heat the oil to 350°F for your favorite method of deep-frying. One piece at a time, dust a shrimp with cornstarch, then place it lightly in the egg wash, then roll it in the cracker-crumb mixture. Fry the shrimp in the hot oil until done; they will float to the top when cooked through. Remove the shrimp when done with a slotted spoon and place them on paper towels to drain.

YIELD: 4 SERVINGS

Honey BBQ Strips

These chicken strips are easy to make with a little elbow grease. You can make a large batch of these up fresh for a ball game, tailgate party, or even a family night in. In this recipe, you make battered chicken strips, and then add a few extra ingredients to the store-bought barbecue sauce. I think you will find that these taste very close to the original.

CHICKEN STRIPS:
8 cups vegetable oil, for deep-frying

2¾ cups flour

1 teaspoon salt

1 teaspoon freshly ground pepper

1 cup buttermilk

2 pounds boneless, skinless chicken breast strips

BBQ SAUCE:
1 cup hickory smoked barbecue sauce (like Heinz)

¼ cup water

2 tablespoons honey

1 tablespoon ketchup

1 teaspoon liquid smoke

FOR CHICKEN STRIPS: Heat the oil in a large pot or deep-fryer to 375°F. Mix the flour, salt, and pepper in a bowl and set aside. Place the buttermilk in a separate bowl. Dip the chicken strips in the flour mixture, then in the buttermilk, and then finally in the flour again. Place the strips into the hot oil (don't overcrowd them). Fry until lightly golden brown. Remove the strips from the oil and drain them on paper towels.

FOR BBQ SAUCE: Place all the ingredients in a small saucepan. Mix the sauce thoroughly and let it simmer on low heat, stirring frequently, for 20 minutes. Preheat the oven to 350°F. After 20 minutes of simmering, let the sauce cool slightly, then dip one chicken strip at a time in the sauce and place them in a baking pan that has been sprayed lightly with a nonstick spray. Bake the strips for 20 minutes. Serve with your favorite side dishes or pack up a few things and have a picnic in the backyard.

YIELD: 4 SERVINGS

CopyKat.com's **LOGAN FARMS**

Honey Glazed Ham®

Ham encrusted with a sweet and almost spicy layer will delight you and your guests during your next get-together. The glaze will cook on the outside of the ham and give it a whole new flavor.

1 (10-pound) ham, precooked or partially cooked	⅛ teaspoon ground allspice
½ cup honey	½ to ¾ pound raw sugar (unrefined)

Pierce the ham skin about ⅛-inch deep, about ¼-inch apart, all over the ham. This step may be omitted if the ham is spiral-cut. Mix the honey with the allspice. Place the sliced side of the ham down on the baking tray. Pour the honey mixture over the ham, making sure that it is covered completely. Place the ham in the refrigerator, uncovered, for 2 hours. Then remove the ham from the refrigerator and cover it with the sugar. Place the ham back in the refrigerator for 30 minutes and preheat the oven according to the directions on the ham. Bake the ham uncovered according to the directions if partially cooked, or bake until heated through, if it's precooked.

YIELD: 20 SERVINGS

Chicken Durango

Cafeteria food often gets labeled as less-than-flavorful, but Luby's™ is an exception to that way of thinking. This is a creative way to serve chicken breasts: They're coated with bread crumbs and stuffed them with ham and Swiss cheese. If you have some leftover ham from another recipe, you can use it in place of the deli-sliced ham.

4 boneless, skinless
chicken breasts

1 teaspoon seasoned salt

¼ teaspoon pepper

1½ cups plain bread crumbs

about 2 tablespoons vegetable oil

1 cup milk

⅓ cup tartar sauce
(like Hellmann's)

4 (1-ounce) pieces thinly sliced
lean ham

4 (1-ounce) pieces processed
Swiss cheese

Pound the chicken breasts flat by covering each one with plastic wrap and using a mallet to pound each one to ½-inch thick. Mix the seasoned salt, pepper, and bread crumbs together, and set aside. In a frying pan on medium heat, heat just enough vegetable oil to cover the bottom of the pan. Dust the chicken breasts with the bread crumb mixture, dip them in the milk, then dip them back in the bread crumbs. Place the chicken in the preheated pan and fry the breasts until golden brown. Remove the chicken breasts and place them on a serving tray. Spread 1½ tablespoons tartar sauce on each chicken breast. Place a slice of ham on each breast. Top the ham with a slice of Swiss cheese. Place the chicken in the oven or microwave just long enough to heat and melt the cheese. Serve with your favorite salad or side vegetable.

NOTE: To help cut down the cooking time, I highly recommend pounding out the chicken breasts and making them thinner. Plus, if you are trying to save calories, this helps you feel like you've received a larger piece of meat than you actually have.

YIELD: 4 SERVINGS

CopyKat.com's **LUBY'S™**

Italian Chicken Breast

Boneless, skinless chicken breasts are a staple of many meals, We coat these scrumptious Italian-inspired chicken breasts with Italian seasonings, Parmesan cheese, and mozzarella. These reheat well if you add the mozzarella cheese just before serving.

1 pound (4 cups) shredded mozzarella cheese, plus extra for garnish

3 cups flour, divided

¼ cup dried parsley flakes

⅓ cup grated Parmesan cheese

1 (0.7-ounce) package dry Italian salad dressing mix

1 cup milk

2 extra-large eggs

8 boneless, skinless chicken breasts

2 tablespoons vegetable oil

¼ cup chopped fresh parsley, for garnish

In a medium-size bowl, combine the mozzarella, 2 cups flour, parsley flakes, Parmesan cheese and the Italian salad dressing mix; blend well. In a shallow bowl, whisk together the milk and eggs until well blended. Place the remaining 1 cup flour in another shallow bowl. Coat each chicken breast with the plain flour, shaking off any excess, then dip it into the milk mixture, then into the cheese mixture, coating evenly and pressing the cheese into the chicken. Heat about ⅛-inch oil in large skillet over medium heat. Add the chicken breasts and cook for 5 to 6 minutes on each side, or until cooked through. Garnish with mozzarella cheese and parsley.

YIELD: 8 SERVINGS

Mesquite Chicken

This is a delicious recipe. Be warned: It's very filling. In this recipe that is similar to Mason Jar's™, you have pineapple chunks, mushroom pieces, ham, cheese, and more. This is a great recipe to make ahead and warm up when you're ready to serve it.

1 (8-ounce) can pineapple chunks	1 (8-ounce) jar broiled mushroom pieces (see note)
4 boneless, skinless chicken breasts, flattened	1 pound deli-sliced honey ham
12 ounces mesquite cooking sauce and marinade	4 thick slices Monterey Jack cheese

Pour the pineapple juice into a large skillet and add the chicken breasts. Cook the chicken over medium-high heat until the breasts are no longer pink in the middle, about 5 to 7 minutes on each side. Preheat the oven to 350°F. Remove the meat from the skillet and discard the juices. Arrange the breasts in a large casserole dish. Pour the mesquite marinade over all the chicken breasts. Evenly divide the mushrooms on the top of each chicken breast, and then evenly divide the ham on top. Top each breast with a thick slice of Monterey Jack cheese. Bake the chicken for about 10 minutes, or until the cheese is melted. (You can also do this step in the microwave. It takes about 2 minutes on high power.)

NOTE: You can use fresh mushrooms for this recipe if you like. Sliced mushrooms are sold in the grocery store in 8-ounce packages. Sauté one package of sliced mushrooms with 2 tablespoons of butter over medium heat in a large saucepan. Season the mushrooms with ½ teaspoon salt. The mushrooms are cooked when they have browned and reduced in size by two-thirds.

YIELD: 4 SERVINGS

CopyKat.com's **MCALISTER'S DELI®**

Beef and Cheddar Spud

Sometimes there is nothing better than a baked potato to fill you up. So often we make baked potatoes and serve them up with butter, sour cream, and little else. These potatoes are made with cheddar cheese, thickly sliced roast beef, and gravy.

2 russet baking potatoes

¼ cup thickly sliced deli roast beef

½ cup shredded cheddar cheese

½ cup canned beef gravy

Preheat the oven to 350°F. Bake the potatoes for about 45 minutes or until they are done; test them for doneness by piercing them with a fork. Slice the end off one side of each of the potatoes. Arrange the potatoes together by lining up the cut ends, and split them open lengthwise across the top. Roughly chop the roast beef into ½-inch pieces—you want the meat nice and chunky—and place it on the potatoes. Cover the potatoes with cheese and place them back into the oven until the cheese is melted. While the cheese is melting, heat up the beef gravy. Remove the potatoes from the oven, and place them on a serving dish. Serve the potatoes with beef gravy poured on top. Optional toppings could be sour cream, chopped red onion, or chopped green onion.

YIELD: 1 LARGE SERVING

Pasta Alfredo

★ ⏲ 🌱

This was the recipe that spawned my desire to re-create restaurant-style dishes. At my first spoonful, I was hooked on this warm pasta covered in cream sauce with cheese and hint of garlic. Honestly, if I am in the Olive Garden®, I always at least consider ordering it. My big tip for this recipe is to use good-quality Parmesan cheese; forgo the kind that you get in the green container and use some freshly grated cheese if possible. The kind in the green can doesn't melt well, and you won't get good results with it.

½ pound dry pasta (your choice)	2 cups (1 pint) heavy cream
½ cup (1 stick) butter	¾ cup Parmesan cheese
1 teaspoon garlic powder	

Cook the pasta according to the package directions. In a saucepan over medium heat, combine the butter and garlic powder, and heat just until the butter begins to bubble. Then add the heavy cream and cook until the whole mixture beings to bubble, then add the Parmesan cheese. Stir frequently while the cheese melts. Once the cheese has melted, turn down the heat and simmer until ready to serve.

There are two ways to serve Alfredo sauce. The Olive Garden serves their sauce ladled over a mound of pasta, but the traditional Italian way is to pour all of the pasta into a bowl and then pour all of the sauce over top the cooked pasta and mix thoroughly. If you want to save your sauce and pasta for another meal, I recommend serving the pasta and sauce separately, but if you plan on eating all of the pasta at a single sitting, the traditional Italian way is fantastic.

YIELD: 4 SERVINGS

CopyKat.com's **OLIVE GARDEN®**

Capellini Pomodoro

Olive Garden® is known for their delicious pasta and for making you feel like family. Why not bring some of that feeling home with this light, healthy Capellini Pomodoro? You can make this dish when you have barely anything in your kitchen. Fresh vine-ripened tomatoes, fresh basil, garlic, and pasta make a filling and flavorful meal.

12 ounces dry capellini pasta

⅓ cup extra-virgin olive oil

2 cloves garlic, minced

2 pounds plum tomatoes, seeded and diced

¼ teaspoon pepper

1 tablespoon fresh basil leaves, minced

3 tablespoons grated Parmesan cheese, divided

Prepare the pasta according to the package directions. While the pasta is cooking, heat the olive oil and add the garlic; cook until the garlic turns white, about 2 minutes. Add the tomatoes and pepper and heat through, stirring constantly, about 2 to 3 minutes. The tomatoes should not lose their shape. Remove the pan from the heat. Transfer the hot, cooked pasta to a large bowl. Toss the pasta gently with the tomato mixture, basil, and half of the Parmesan cheese. Serve immediately and top with the remaining Parmesan.

YIELD: 4 SERVINGS

Capellini Primavera

This is a light and wonderful dish if you're watching what you're eating. It's full of vegetables and not overly heavy. Fresh carrots, mushrooms, and broccoli help make for a healthy dinner.

1 pound fresh (or 8 ounces dry) capellini pasta

½ cup (1 stick) butter

1½ cups chopped onions

¾ cup julienne-cut carrots

1 pound broccoli florets, cut into 1-inch pieces

2 cloves garlic, minced

8 ounces (2 cups) sliced mushrooms

1¼ cups thinly sliced yellow summer squash (cut in half lengthwise before slicing)

1 tablespoon beef bouillon granules (or vegetable broth)

¼ cup sun-dried tomatoes, oil-packed, minced

1 (14-ounce) can crushed tomatoes, in purée

1 tablespoon chopped fresh parsley

¼ teaspoon dried oregano

¼ teaspoon dried rosemary

¼ teaspoon crushed dried rosemary

1½ cups water

½ cup shredded Parmesan cheese

Prepare the pasta according to the package directions. While the pasta is cooking, you can prepare the remainder of the dish. In a large, heavy pan, melt the butter over medium heat and sauté the onions, carrots, broccoli, and garlic for about 5 minutes. Be careful not to let the garlic become too brown and burn. Then add the mushrooms and squash and sauté for an additional 2 minutes. Add the bouillon granules, sun-dried tomatoes, crushed tomatoes, parsley, oregano, rosemary, and water to the pan and cook for approximately 10 minutes so all the flavors are well incorporated. Spoon the sauce over the cooked pasta and add the Parmesan cheese on top.

YIELD: 4 LARGE SERVINGS

CopyKat.com's **OLIVE GARDEN**®

Chicken Marsala

★

Chicken Marsala is one of my favorite Italian dishes. This chicken is lightly dredged in seasoned flour, then browned in a pan. The pan drippings from the chicken and caramelized bits of buttery mushrooms and onions make a thick and flavorful sauce. This is one recipe where I suggest you use a dry Marsala wine; the sweet style of this wine doesn't have as hearty and rich a flavor as the dry does.

¼ cup cake flour

½ teaspoon salt

½ teaspoon pepper

½ teaspoon dried oregano

4 tablespoons oil

4 tablespoons butter

4 boneless, skinless chicken breasts

1 cup sliced fresh mushrooms

½ cup dry Marsala wine

Combine the flour, salt, pepper, and oregano and blend well. Heat the oil and butter in a skillet until it's bubbling lightly. Dredge the chicken in the flour mixture and shake off the excess. Cook the chicken in the pan for about 2 minutes on the first side, until lightly brown. As you turn the breasts to the second side to cook, add the mushrooms around the chicken. Cook about 2 more minutes, until the chicken is lightly browned on the second side. Stir the mushrooms. When the second side is lightly browned, add the wine, cover the pan and simmer for about 10 minutes.

YIELD: 4 SERVINGS

Parmesan-Crusted Chicken Breast and Bow-Tie Pasta

★ 🍳

Often the Olive Garden® has a very seasonal menu, serving up fabulous dishes only for a short period of time. Here is one of my personal favorites that they have served in the past. Chicken breasts are dredged in seasoned bread crumbs and Parmesan cheese. Then as the cheese cooks inside the crust it becomes almost pungent, with a nutty flavor. We combine this with a creamy sauce served over bow-tie pasta.

2 cups dry bow-tie pasta

6 boneless, skinless chicken breasts

4 cups vegetable oil (for frying)

1 cup plain bread crumbs

4 tablespoons flour, divided

¼ cup Parmesan cheese

1 cup milk

2 tablespoons butter

3 tablespoons olive oil

2 teaspoons crushed garlic

¼ cup water

½ teaspoon salt

½ cup white table wine

¾ cup half-and-half

¼ cup sour cream

¾ cup finely grated mild Asiago cheese

4 tablespoons fresh basil leaves

4 broccoli florets, lightly steamed, for garnish

2 white mushrooms, quartered, lightly steamed, for garnish

¼ teaspoon crushed red pepper, for garnish

Prepare the pasta according to the package directions. Wash and drain the chicken breasts. Pound the chicken breasts flat by covering them with plastic wrap and using a mallet to flatten the breasts to ½-inch thick. Heat the oil to 350°F in a deep pan. Mix the bread crumbs, 2 tablespoons flour, and the Parmesan cheese together. Place the milk in a separate dish. Dip the chicken in the bread crumb mixture, then in the milk, and then back in the bread crumbs. Place the breasts in the hot oil and fry until golden. Remove and drain the chicken.

In a saucepan on medium heat, melt the butter and add the olive oil. Whisk in the remaining 2 tablespoons of flour until the mixture is blended. Quickly add the garlic, water, and salt and stir well. Add the wine and stir well. Immediately add the half-and-half and sour cream and stir. When the mixture is smooth, add the Asiago cheese and stir until melted. Finally, sprinkle the fresh basil in the sauce, stir gently, and remove the pan from the heat.

To assemble each serving, place 2 cups cooked pasta in an individual pasta dish. Spoon about ½ to ¾ cup sauce over the pasta, then add the broccoli and mushrooms. Place the Parmesan chicken over the pasta and sprinkle crushed red pepper and Parmesan cheese on top, if desired.

∞∞∞∞∞∞∞∞∞∞∞∞∞∞∞∞∞∞∞∞∞∞∞∞∞∞∞∞

YIELD: 6 SERVINGS

Shrimp Christopher

Pasta and shrimp served in a basil-butter sauce is not only easy to make, but it tastes great. You can have dinner done in minutes with this recipe.

2 ounces fresh basil leaves (about 2 bunches)

1¼ cups (2½ sticks) butter, softened

1 teaspoon minced garlic

¼ teaspoon salt

⅛ teaspoon black pepper

3 tablespoons shredded Parmesan cheese, plus additional for garnish

1 tablespoon shredded Romano cheese

1 pound fresh linguine or angel-hair pasta

1 pound medium shrimp, shelled and deveined

Remove any large stems from the basil and wash the leaves. Shake off any excess water and dry them with a paper towel. Place the leaves in the food processor and process until finely chopped, doing it in two batches if necessary to get it uniformly chopped. Place the butter in a small mixing bowl. Using an electric mixer, whip the butter until pliable. Add the garlic, salt, pepper, Parmesan and Romano cheeses, and the chopped basil; mix until well incorporated. This basil butter can be used immediately or stored, covered in the refrigerator, for three to four days. Prepare the pasta according to the package directions, drain well, and keep warm. Melt the basil butter in a large skillet over medium heat. Add the shrimp and sauté until just done, about 2 to 3 minutes. Serve over the hot pasta. Garnish with freshly grated Parmesan cheese.

YIELD: 4 SERVINGS

Alice Springs Chicken®

★

One of my favorite menu items at Outback Steakhouse™ has always been their Alice Springs Chicken®: grilled chicken breasts topped with honey mustard, bacon, and cheese!

4 (½-inch thick) boneless, skinless chicken breasts

½ teaspoon seasoned salt, like Morton's SeasonAll

6 strips of bacon, cut in half

2 tablespoons oil

½ cup honey mustard

1 cup sliced mushrooms (canned or in a jar), drained

3 cups shredded Colby Jack cheese

parsley, for garnish

Rub the chicken breasts with the seasoned salt and set aside to marinate for 1 hour. While the breasts are marinating, fry the bacon until it's crisp, then drain.

Heat the oil, just enough to prevent the chicken from sticking, in a pan on medium heat and sauté the marinated chicken. Cook on both sides until the breasts turn a slight golden color and are cooked in the middle but not dry, about 5 to 7 minutes on each side. Transfer the chicken from the pan to a cookie sheet.

Preheat the oven to 350°F. Spread the chicken breasts with a tablespoon each of honey mustard, cover them with a layer of mushrooms and three pieces of bacon and then cover with the shredded Colby Jack cheese. Pop the pan in the preheated oven, or a microwave, just until the cheese melts, about 1 to 2 minutes. Sprinkle with parsley. Extra honey mustard can be served on the side.

YIELD: 4 SERVINGS

Queensland Chicken and Shrimp

You might not think of Outback Steakhouse™ having a pasta dish that is just fabulous, but they do. Combining a cream sauce with chicken, shrimp, and pasta makes for an intriguing combination.

¼ teaspoon poultry seasoning

⅛ to ¼ teaspoon cayenne pepper, to taste

⅛ teaspoon white pepper

⅛ teaspoon onion powder

1 tablespoon garlic powder

½ cup milk

2 tablespoons butter

1 cup heavy cream

1 pound dry linguine

1 tablespoon olive oil

4 chicken breasts

½ cup dry white wine

8 ounces medium shrimp

In a small bowl, combine the poultry seasoning, cayenne pepper, white pepper, onion powder, and garlic powder and mix well. In a large skillet, combine the milk, half of the spice mixture, butter, and cream and heat on high until the mixture bubbles, then reduce the heat. The cream mixture will thicken; let it reduce by 20 percent, then set aside until later. Cook the linguine to the al dente stage, according to the package directions. In a skillet, add the olive oil and sauté the chicken breasts, seasoning them with the remaining spice mixture. Cook the chicken for approximately 5 to 7 minutes on each side, until it has browned. Remove the chicken breasts from the pan and place them either in a warm oven or on a dish, covered with foil, so the chicken doesn't get cold while you prepare the shrimp. Pour the wine into the pan, then add the shrimp and sauté. Serve each breast on a bed of linguine with shrimp. Cover with sauce.

YIELD: 4 SERVINGS

Caribou Coconut Chicken

The Rainforest Cafe® is a fun place to go, and the jungle setting can really whet the appetite. The coconut in their tasty chicken tenders adds a sweet and crispy touch that is just right!

1½ pounds boneless, skinless chicken breast, ⅓ to½-inch thick	¼ cup flour
	2 eggs, beaten
2 teaspoons sugar	¼ cup water
2 teaspoons salt	8 cups vegetable oil, for deep-frying
2 cups flaked coconut	
1 cup cornstarch	1 ripe pineapple

Trim the chicken breasts so the pieces measure about 4 x 2½ inches. Sprinkle the sugar and salt over the chicken breasts, place them in a Ziploc bag, and let them marinate in the refrigerator for 4 hours.

When the chicken breasts have marinated, rinse them lightly and drain. In a large pot or deep-fryer, heat the oil to 350°F. Place the coconut, cornstarch, and flour in a bowl and mix well. In a separate bowl, place the beaten eggs, add the water, and blend well. Dip the chicken breasts in the egg wash and then place them in the coconut mixture and coat well. Carefully place the chicken in the hot oil and cook until lightly golden. Remove and place on a paper towel. When frying chicken, do not crowd the pan and keep a check on the oil so it does not burn.

Slice a ripe pineapple in ⅛-inch rounds and cut the rounds in half. Spray a nonstick saucepan with nonstick spray and lightly sauté the pineapple just until heated through. The pineapple will turn a more intense yellow. Serve it the pineapple on the side of the chicken with Rainforest Cafe Honey Mustard Dipping Sauce (page 248). The coconut chicken at the Rainforest Cafe was served with the sauce on top, but I've elected to serve the sauce on the side for presentation.

YIELD: 4 SERVINGS

Cajun Shrimp

Red Lobster® made these barbecue-style shrimp for one of their unlimited shrimp feasts. Barbecue-style is a spicy and buttery Cajun way to easily make a unique shrimp dish. Now, that doesn't mean the shrimp is covered with barbecue sauce; rather, it is baked in the oven in a spicy sauce. Be sure to serve this with rice or plenty of bread so you can mop up the extra sauce.

½ cup margarine (see note)

1 pound medium or large shrimp

2 teaspoons cayenne pepper

3 teaspoons salt

2 teaspoons black pepper

2 teaspoons paprika

2 teaspoons cumin

2¼ teaspoons dry mustard

1 teaspoon dried thyme

1 teaspoon dried oregano

2 teaspoons onion powder

2 teaspoons garlic powder

lemon wedges, for garnish

Preheat the oven to 400°F. Place the margarine in a 9 x 13-inch baking pan and then place the pan in the oven. While the pan is in the oven, wash, peel, and devein the shrimp. By the time you have finished prepping the shrimp, the margarine should be melted in the pan. In a small bowl, mix together the cayenne pepper, salt, black pepper, paprika, cumin, dry mustard, thyme, oregano, onion powder, and garlic powder and blend well. Place the shrimp into the pan and then sprinkle on the seasoning mixture. Mix the shrimp, margarine, and spices until the shrimp is well coated. Bake for approximately 15 minutes, then remove the shrimp from the oven and check for doneness. The shrimp should be pink when done. Serve with fresh lemon wedges.

NOTE: This recipe uses margarine because most restaurants use it as it is less expensive than butter. If you really want to try to ramp up this recipe, use unsalted butter instead of margarine.

YIELD: 4 SERVINGS

Crab Alfredo

Creamy Alfredo sauce and crab go so well over pasta that you may wonder why you didn't think of this sooner. If you are going to buy crab legs, purchase them either fresh or frozen—do not purchase them in a thawed state. You can easily thaw frozen crab legs by placing them in your refrigerator for about 8 hours before using.

½ cup (1 stick) unsalted butter	1 teaspoon garlic powder
2 tablespoons cream cheese	8 ounces dry fettuccine pasta
2 cups (1 pint) half-and-half	4 to 6 crab legs
½ to ¾ cup Parmesan cheese	1 teaspoon salt

In a saucepan, melt the butter, then add the cream cheese. When the cream cheese is softened, add the half-and-half and the Parmesan cheese. Add the garlic powder and stir well. Simmer the sauce for 15 to 20 minutes on low heat. You may wish to season it with a little salt and pepper. Prepare the pasta according to the package directions. Prepare the crab legs by cooking them in a large pot of boiling water seasoned with 1 teaspoon of salt. Cook the crab legs for 5 to 7 minutes, then remove them from the pot of boiling water. Crack open the legs, lightly dry off the excess water with a paper towel, and place the crab on top of the Alfredo sauce and pasta.

YIELD: 4 SERVINGS

Parrot Isle Coconut Shrimp

If you have never had coconut shrimp, you have been missing out!
Lightly battered shrimp encased in a crispy coconut batter will
immediately transport you to a tropical island.

8 cups vegetable oil,
for deep-frying

1 cup plain bread crumbs

¾ cup cornstarch, divided

1 cup sweetened coconut flakes

½ cup piña colada mix
(Major Peters' is my favorite)

1 tablespoon powdered sugar

3 tablespoons spiced rum
(like Captain Morgan).

½ pounds large shrimp, cleaned,
peeled, and butterflied

In a large pot or deep-fryer, heat the vegetable oil to 375°F. Mix the bread
crumbs, ¼ cup cornstarch, and coconut in a deep bowl and set aside. Combine
the piña colada mix, powdered sugar, and rum in a small mixing bowl and set
aside. Place the remaining ½ cup cornstarch in a separate bowl. Coat the shrimp
first in the cornstarch, then into the piña colada mixture, then dust the shrimp in
the bread crumb mixture. For a second coating, place the shrimp back into the
piña colada mix, then into the cornstarch mixture, and finally the bread crumb
mixture. Place the prepared shrimp carefully into the hot oil. Fry until golden
brown, remove from the fryer, and drain. Serve with Red Lobster's Piña Colada
Dipping Sauce (page 249).

YIELD: 1 MAIN DISH SERVING OR 2 APPETIZER SERVINGS

Shrimp Scampi

Shrimp scampi is a wonderful dish in which the shrimp is gently cooked in a butter-and-garlic-infused sauce. The flavors blend beautifully together, and I suggest serving this over a bed of rice so you don't miss a drop of the sauce.

½ cup (1 stick) unsalted butter (do not use margarine)

3 teaspoons minced garlic

1 cup dry white wine

1 pound shrimp, peeled and deveined

Preheat the oven to 350°F. In a small saucepan, melt the butter, add the minced garlic then add the white wine. Whisk the butter and wine mixture together. Place the shrimp in a 1-quart casserole dish and pour the butter mixture over the shrimp. Bake for about 6 to 7 minutes. Be careful not to overcook the shrimp. The shrimp is done when it has turned pink.

YIELD: 2 SERVINGS

Fritos® Chili Cheese Wrap

★ ⏱

Going to Sonic® while growing up was always a real treat. One of my friends or I got the car, and what better place to go than to the drive-in? I still go there sometimes, even if it's not just to check out who else is there. Their Fritos® Chili Cheese Wrap is easy to make and tastes great. If you are a fan of Fritos® Pies, you will enjoy this recipe.

1 (19-ounce) can chili
(my favorite is Hormel, no beans)

4 flour tortillas

2 cups Fritos chips

¼ cup diced red onions

½ cup shredded cheddar cheese

Heat the chili until it's warm. Warm the tortillas in the microwave for about 30 seconds to make them pliable. If they are stale, you can sprinkle a little water on them before they go in the microwave to help freshen them up. Place ½ cup Fritos in each tortilla, add a ladle of chili, and sprinkle on the red onions and cheddar cheese. Roll them up like burritos and enjoy.

YIELD: 4 SERVINGS

Mexican Pizza

Taco Bell® makes so many different menu items, and who would have thought you could find a pizza in a Mexican restaurant? Here, a pizza is built on a crispy flour tortilla that is stacked with sauce, meat, cheese, and fresh veggies.

1 cup vegetable oil

12 (6 to 7-inch) flour tortillas

1 (14-ounce) can refried beans

1 recipe Taco Bell Seasoned Meat (page 136)

1 recipe Taco Bell Mild Sauce (page 253)

1 (12-ounce) package shredded Monterey Jack/cheddar cheese mix

2 to 3 small Roma tomatoes, diced

3 to 5 green onion tops, diced

In a shallow frying pan, add the oil, and heat the oil to 350°F. Fry each tortilla in the oil, turning the tortilla over as it browns. This will happen very quickly, and should take about 30 seconds for each side. Drain the tortillas on paper towels.

To assemble each pizza, use:

one fried tortilla

spread 2 tablespoons of refried beans

spoon 2 tablespoons of seasoned taco meat

one fried tortilla

spread 2 tablespoons of taco sauce

sprinkle 3 tablespoons of cheese on top

Pop the pizza into the microwave and heat until the cheese is melted, about 1 minute at high power. Sprinkle 1 tablespoon diced tomatoes and 1 tablespoon diced green onions on top of each pizza. Serve and enjoy!

YIELD: 6 PIZZAS

Seasoned Meat

Taco Bell® does wonders with a few basic ingredients. This meat is one of their critical ingredients to make other dishes and will have you making tacos, burritos, and nachos in no time. You may not be familiar with the masa harina, but you'll find this corn flour in the baking section near the flour in your grocery store. Wonder what to do with the rest of the masa? Try making the Chili's® Chicken Enchilada Soup (page 77).

1½ tablespoons masa harina

4½ teaspoons chili powder

½ teaspoon onion powder

½ teaspoon garlic powder

½ teaspoon seasoned salt

½ teaspoon paprika

½ teaspoon cumin

½ teaspoon garlic salt

¼ teaspoon sugar

1 teaspoon dried minced onion

1⅓ pounds ground beef chuck

¾ to 1 cup water

In a small bowl, mix together all of the ingredients except the meat and water. Stir the spice mixture well, making sure that all the spices have been blended. Crumble the ground beef into a frying pan and brown the meat, stirring well. Remove the beef from the heat, place the meat into a sieve and rinse it with hot water, then drain the water and grease from the beef. Return the beef to the pan and add the spice mix. Add the water to the ground beef and seasoning and simmer on medium-low heat for 20 minutes, until most of the moisture has cooked away. Remove from the heat when the moisture in the meat has dissipated but the meat is not dry.

YIELD: ENOUGH MEAT FOR ABOUT 12 TACOS

Jack Daniel's® Grill Glaze

There is only one problem with this sauce: You can never get enough of it. This grill glaze is wonderful to pour over meat, to dip a sandwich in, or to finish cooking your favorite meat on the grill. I especially like it with chicken fingers or crispy, deep-fried chicken breast strips.

1/3 cup diced red onion

1/2 teaspoon finely diced garlic

1/2 cup water

1/2 cup brown sugar

1/3 cup teriyaki sauce

1/4 cup soy sauce

1/3 cup white grape juice

1/2 cup Jack Daniel's Black Label Bourbon

1/2 teaspoon Tabasco sauce

Place the pan on medium heat and add all the ingredients to the pan in the order listed, stirring after each addition. Continue stirring until the mixture reaches a boil. Then turn the temperature down to low until the mixture is on a slow simmer. Cook the sauce for 35 to 45 minutes, until it has reduced in volume by about 25 percent, then remove from the heat.

YIELD: APPROXIMATELY 3 CUPS

Side Dishes

×××

Sides dishes are what make a meal special for friends and family and can make an ordinary meal extraordinary. It would be difficult to imagine a feast like Thanksgiving without the traditional side dishes. Here we offer you many sides that may become some of your Thanksgiving favorites, like creamy, filling garlic mashed potatoes, a carrot pudding that everyone will quickly gobble down, and a dish similar to Boston Market's® Sweet Potato Casserole.

Sides can be wonderful slow-cooked treats that you bake in the oven, as well as others that you quickly prepare to eat with a hamburger. You may even want to make an entire meal out of several side dishes—many popular restaurants offer a side-only option.

Garlic Mashed Potatoes

Some people feel passionate about their mashed potatoes, and these people are going to be thrilled with this dish. Two changes from standard mashed potatoes make these extra special: I use red potatoes for their unique flavor, and I infuse them with a touch of roasted garlic flavor. To really get the full flavor, the potatoes are baked, not boiled.

1 pound red potatoes	3 tablespoons butter
1 head garlic	¼ cup half-and-half
1 tablespoon olive oil	salt and pepper, to taste

Preheat the oven to 350°F. Bake the potatoes for 20 to 30 minutes. This is also a great time to roast that garlic, too. You can either use a traditional garlic roaster, if you have one, or you can coat a head of garlic with the olive oil, wrap it in foil, and roast it in the oven with the potatoes. The garlic will take about 20 minutes to roast. You'll know it's done because the bulb will give when squeezed.

Remove the potatoes from the oven and allow them to cool. You can leave the skin on or off the potatoes; I like to leave a few of them on because they add a nice variety of flavor. Chop the potatoes into 1-inch cubes, add the butter and half-and-half, and mix everything together with an electric mixer. Add 4 cloves of roasted garlic, and salt and pepper to taste. It is best to leave the potatoes a little chunky; you don't want them to be puréed. You will want to reheat these mashed potatoes in a saucepan until they warm up again.

YIELD: 6 SERVINGS

CopyKat.com's BLACK-EYED PEA™
Squash Casserole

Black-eyed Pea™ is known for their home-style food, and when you go in there, memories come flooding in of dinners spent with close family. This squash casserole is what you want to make after you go to your farmers market. Fresh yellow squash is baked with onions and sprinkled with buttery bread crumbs.

5 pounds medium yellow summer squash

2 eggs, beaten

1 cup bread crumbs, plus additional for topping

½ cup butter

¼ cup sugar

2 tablespoons chopped onion

1 teaspoon salt

dash of pepper

Bring a large pot filled about ⅓ full of water to a boil. Cut the tips off the squash and slice each squash into ½-inch rounds. Drop the squash into the boiling water; there should be enough water to cover the squash; if not, add enough water to cover it completely. Return the water to a boil, reduce the heat, and cook the squash until tender, about 15 minutes. Drain the squash in a colander, move the pieces back to the pot, and mash the squash.

Preheat the oven to 350°F. Add to the squash the beaten eggs, 1 cup bread crumbs, butter, sugar, onion, salt, and pepper. Transfer the mixture into a 3-quart casserole dish that has been lightly sprayed with a nonstick spray. Cover the top with a light layer of bread crumbs. Bake for 20 to 25 minutes or until lightly browned.

YIELD: 12 SERVINGS

CopyKat.com's **BOSTON MARKET®**

Cornbread ✓

This is a sweet cornbread that everyone will love. Honestly, I have taken this cornbread to gatherings, and there has never been any left over. The sweet, grainy, dense bread goes well with a warm bowl of soup or beans, or is delicious just by itself.

> 1 (8½-ounce) box Jiffy Mix Corn
> Muffin Mix
> 1 (9-ounce) box Jiffy Mix Golden Yellow
> Cake Mix or regular yellow cake mix

Preheat the oven to 350°F. Mix both boxes of cake and bread mix according to the directions on the package. I generally use a large mixing bowl, combine both boxes together, and then add the other ingredients listed on the packages all at once. If you have only boxes of Jiffy Mix, use a brownie-sized 8 x 8-inch baking pan; if you are going to use one box of regular cake mix, use a 9 x 13-inch pan. Bake for about 30 minutes. When a toothpick inserted into the center of the bread comes out clean, you know it's done.

YIELD: 24 SERVINGS

Creamed Spinach

Growing up, many of us associated spinach with punishment. Sure, Popeye might have eaten spinach, but when it came out of a can, it didn't have a lot of appeal. This creamed spinach recipe will have those who don't enjoy creamed spinach wondering how they lived without this spectacular dish. Creamed spinach is made by using frozen spinach and making a silky smooth sauce.

WHITE SAUCE:
3 tablespoons butter
4 tablespoons flour
¼ teaspoon salt
1 cup whole milk

SPINACH:
2 tablespoons butter
2 tablespoons finely chopped onion
1 (20-ounce) package frozen chopped spinach
¼ cup water
1 teaspoon salt
1 cup White Sauce (see recipe below)
½ cup sour cream

FOR WHITE SAUCE: Over medium-low heat, melt the butter in a saucepan. Add the flour and salt and whisk until they are creamed together. Increase the heat to medium and add the milk a little at a time. Constantly stir with a whisk until the mixture becomes thick and smooth. Remove the sauce from the heat and set it aside.

FOR SPINACH: Place the butter in a 2-quart saucepan on medium heat and add the onions. Cook until the onions are transparent. Add the spinach and the water to the pan, lower the heat, and place a lid on the pan. Stir several times until the spinach is almost completely cooked, about 10 minutes. Add the salt. When the spinach is done, add the prepared White Sauce and sour cream, stir well, and allow the spinach to simmer until completely blended.

YIELD: 8 SERVINGS

Dill Potato Wedges

Potatoes are one of the most satisfying side dishes imaginable. Here we use small red potatoes known for their tender and sweet flesh. They are boiled and then tossed into a bowl with a butter-and-herb infused sauce.

7 or 8 red new potatoes

½ cup (1 stick) butter
(use only real butter)

2 cloves garlic, finely minced

½ teaspoon salt

½ teaspoon black pepper

½ teaspoon celery salt

2 teaspoons crushed dried dill
(or 4 teaspoons fresh dill)

Bring a large pot of water to a boil. Wash the potatoes well and boil them in the water until soft, then drain well on paper towels. Cut the potatoes into 6 or 8 wedges, depending upon the size of the potato. Melt the butter in a large frying pan and sauté the garlic for a couple of moments, and then add the potatoes, salt, pepper, celery salt, and dill. Pan-fry the potatoes until they are light brown.

YIELD: 4 SERVINGS

Macaroni and Cheese

Can you really make a list of comfort foods and not include macaroni and cheese? Rotini, otherwise known as spiral pasta, is one of the trademarks of the Boston Market® macaroni and cheese. We start out with spiral pasta and then surround it with a creamy cheese sauce complete with a touch of onion and dry mustard.

6 ounces dry rotini pasta	2 cups milk
¼ cup butter	1 cup processed American cheese
1 tablespoon minced onion	(Velveeta is best for this dish)
¼ cup flour	1 teaspoon salt, or to taste
¼ teaspoon dry mustard	dash of pepper, to taste

Cook the pasta according to the package instructions, drain, and set aside. To make the cheese sauce, melt the butter in a saucepan, add the onion, and cook until the onion is transparent. Add the flour and dry mustard and blend the sauce with a whisk. Cook the flour and butter mixture for at least 1 minute, then slowly add the milk. When all the milk is added, add the cheese. Stir until the cheese is fully melted, and then season the sauce with salt and pepper to your personal preference. In a serving bowl, add the pasta, pour the cheese sauce over the top, and mix well.

YIELD: 8 SERVINGS

Sweet Potato Casserole

★ 🌱

Can you honestly think of Thanksgiving without a sweet potato casserole? In this dish, your spoon cracks through the streusel and melted marshmallows and sinks slowly into the creamy sweet potatoes.

SWEET POTATOES:	OATMEAL STREUSEL:
5 to 6 sweet potatoes	½ cup rolled oats
¾ cup dark brown sugar	4 tablespoons dark brown sugar
½ cup heavy cream	2 tablespoons all-purpose flour
¼ cup melted butter	¼ teaspoon ground cinnamon
¼ teaspoon cinnamon	4 tablespoons cold butter
¼ teaspoon salt	
2 cups miniature marshmallows	

FOR SWEET POTATOES: Preheat the oven to 400°F. Wash the sweet potatoes and bake them for 60 to 70 minutes or until they are tender. When the potatoes are cool enough to handle, scrape out the insides into a large bowl and discard the skins. Use either a stick blender or an electric mixer to mash the potatoes until they are smooth. Measure out 6 cups of the mashed potatoes into a separate large bowl.

Add the brown sugar, heavy cream, melted butter, cinnamon, and salt to the sweet potatoes and mix well with the stick blender or mixer until all the ingredients are incorporated. Pour this mixture into an 8 x 8-inch baking dish. Preheat the oven to 350°F and prepare the Oatmeal Streusel.

FOR OATMEAL STREUSEL: Using a food processor or a blender, process the oats until they become a fine flour. Combine this oat flour with the brown sugar, flour, and cinnamon in a small bowl. Cut the butter into the dry mixture using a fork until you have a crumbly mixture that has pea-sized pieces.

FOR ASSEMBLY: Sprinkle the streusel mixture over the sweet potatoes and bake for 70 to 80 minutes, or until the topping begins to brown. Remove the casserole from the oven and spread the marshmallows evenly across the top.

◇◇◇◇◇◇◇◇◇◇◇◇◇◇◇◇◇◇◇◇◇◇◇◇

YIELD: 8 SERVINGS

CopyKat.com's **CHILI'S®**

Black Beans

Chili's® makes black beans with a little extra kick. Here you enhance plain black beans by adding chili powder and garlic powder. You can serve this versatile dish instead of refried beans, or even use these as the main ingredient in a burrito.

2 (15½-ounce) cans black beans	½ teaspoon chili powder
½ teaspoon sugar	½ teaspoon garlic powder

Combine the black beans, sugar, chili powder, and garlic powder in a saucepan and stir well. Let the beans simmer for about 20 to 25 minutes. You might serve these with a spoonful of pico de gallo on top, or even crushed up tortilla chips.

YIELD: 8 SERVINGS

Cilantro Rice

Chipotle™ makes everything up fresh right in front of you, and their cilantro rice tastes like stepping south of the border. They put their citrus-infused rice speckled with savory cilantro on their famous burritos, but this can also be used as a side dish.

1½ cups white basmati rice

2 teaspoons vegetable oil

2 limes

1¾ cups water

½ teaspoon salt

2 tablespoons freshly chopped cilantro

Rinse the rice in a fine-mesh colander to remove the excess starch that can be left on the grains. Using a medium pot, heat the oil over low and add the rice and the juice of 1 lime and stir. Make sure the rice is glossy with the vegetable oil. Add the water and salt and bring the rice to a rolling boil. Once it is boiling, turn the heat down to low and cook until the rice is tender and all the water is absorbed, about 20 to 25 minutes.

Pour the rice into a bowl, add the cilantro, and sprinkle the juice of the remaining lime over the rice. Fluff the rice with a fork, mixing together the lime juice and cilantro. Salt to your desired taste.

YIELD: 8 SERVINGS

CopyKat.com's CHURCH'S CHICKEN®

Honey-Butter Biscuits

The honey in this delightful recipe adds a perfect touch to your everyday biscuit.

2 cups flour	½ cup vegetable shortening
4 teaspoons baking powder	⅔ cup whole milk
2 teaspoons sugar	¼ cup (½ stick) melted butter, divided
½ teaspoon salt	
1 teaspoon cream of tartar	⅓ cup honey

Preheat the oven to 450°F. Place the flour, baking powder, sugar, salt, and cream of tartar in a mixing bowl. Work in the shortening until the mixture feels like cornmeal. Pour the milk into the dough and mix well. Knead about 12 to 15 times. Break the dough into about 12 pieces, about ¼ to ⅓-cup each. Roll the dough into balls and pat them to ½-inch thick. Brush the balls with about half of the melted butter and place them on a baking sheet. Bake for 10 to 12 minutes.

While the biscuits are in the oven, pour the honey into the remainder of the butter and bring the mixture to a boil; if you feel you need extra butter, it is OK to add a couple more tablespoons. Remove the honey-butter from the heat and set it aside. When the biscuits are done, remove them from the oven and immediately brush them with honey-butter. Serve as a wonderful breakfast or with your favorite fried chicken dinner.

YIELD: 1 DOZEN SMALL BISCUITS

CopyKat.com's **CRACKER BARREL OLD COUNTRY STORE®**

Baby Carrots

Sweet, tender carrots are a perfect addition to any meal, and you can easily make them for dinner. This recipe is made with fresh baby-cut carrots and seasoned with a light touch of brown sugar.

2 pounds fresh baby carrots	1 tablespoon brown sugar
1 teaspoon salt	2 tablespoons margarine

Rinse the carrots and place them in a 2-quart saucepan. Pour enough water in to just cover the top of the carrots. Cover the pan with a lid, place it on medium heat, and bring the water to a boil. Then turn the heat to low and simmer for 30 to 45 minutes until the carrots are tender when pricked with a fork.

Pour half the water off the carrots and add the salt, brown sugar, and margarine. Place the lid on the pan and cook until the carrots are completely tender but not mushy. More salt may be added if needed.

YIELD: 6 SERVINGS

Biscuits

Making biscuits and fried chicken in a local restaurant helped me to pay my way through college, and when I first discovered Cracker Barrel's® dense biscuits, I fell in love with them. Their biscuits are hearty enough to withstand gravy, jelly, honey, or anything else you throw their way.

2¼ cups Bisquick mix	1 teaspoon sugar
⅔ cup buttermilk	1 tablespoon butter, melted

Preheat the oven to 450°F. Mix the Bisquick, buttermilk, and sugar together, then add of the melted butter. Stir the ingredients until a soft dough forms. Turn the dough onto a surface that has been dusted with flour and knead the dough 20 times. Roll the dough out to ½-inch thick and cut the biscuits with a biscuit cutter or a small drinking glass. Place all the biscuits next to each other in an 8 x 8-inch ungreased cake pan, then flatten them slightly. Bake for 8 to 10 minutes.

To make biscuits like Popeye's or KFC's, prepare this recipe, but brush the biscuits with melted butter when they are placed in the oven and again when you take them out of the oven.

YIELD: 12 BISCUITS

CopyKat.com's **CRACKER BARREL OLD COUNTRY STORE®**

Dumplings

★

Soft pillows of dumplings are a delight to eat—filling, and oh so tasty. Growing up I used to angle my soup ladle to fill my bowl with as many steaming dumplings as I could get.

DUMPLINGS:
- 2 quarts (8 cups) water
- 3 chicken bouillon cubes
- 2 cups flour
- 2 teaspoons baking powder
- ½ teaspoon salt
- 1 cup whole milk
- 4 tablespoons vegetable oil

DUMPLING SAUCE:
- 3 tablespoons butter
- ½ teaspoon salt
- 4 tablespoons flour
- 2 chicken bouillon cubes, crumbled
- ½ teaspoon sugar
- 1 cup whole milk

FOR DUMPLINGS: In a large saucepan, bring the water and bouillon cubes to a boil. Make sure the bouillon cubes have dissolved. In a large bowl, mix together the flour, baking powder, salt, milk, and vegetable oil. Blend everything well and turn the dough out onto a floured surface. Knead four or five times and divide the dough into two parts. Roll out one piece of dough to ⅛-inch thick and cut it into 1 x 1½-inch strips. Place the strips into the boiling water and cook the dumplings until they start to float, about 5 to 7 minutes, then remove them from the water with a slotted spoon and set aside. Prepare the remaining dumplings in the same way. While cooking the dumplings, you can prepare the sauce. When all the dumplings are cooked, reserve the cooking liquid.

FOR DUMPLING SAUCE: Melt the butter in a medium saucepan, then add the salt, flour, chicken bouillon cubes, and stir until thick. In a separate bowl, mix the sugar with the milk, and add this mixture to the flour mixture a little at a time; stir constantly with a whisk until it is thick and smooth. Remove the pan from the heat. Add the cooked dumplings to the dumpling sauce and add ½ to ¾ cup of the cooking liquid; this will make the dumplings moist, and the flavor of the bouillon cubes makes them taste very rich.

YIELD: 12 SERVINGS

Fried Apples

When you go to Cracker Barrel®, you simply must have the fried apples, but you really can make them at home. Best of all, apples can be purchased any time of the year at your local grocery store. The apples really aren't fried, but they're cooked in a creamy sauce flavored with brown sugar, cinnamon, and nutmeg. I personally like these best when they're made with bacon drippings, which add a little extra flavor.

¼ cup margarine or bacon drippings

6 tart apples, sliced in ³/₈-inch slices

1 teaspoon lemon juice

¼ cup brown sugar

¹/₈ teaspoon salt

1 teaspoon cinnamon

dash of nutmeg

In a large skillet over low heat, melt the margarine or bacon drippings. Arrange the sliced apples evenly over the skillet bottom. Sprinkle the lemon juice over them, then add the brown sugar and salt. Cover the pan and cook over low heat for 15 minutes until the apples are tender and juicy. Sprinkle with cinnamon and nutmeg.

YIELD: 6 SERVINGS

Green Beans

While we all love a variety of vegetables, green beans have a flavor that is difficult to have too often. Bacon gives the green beans a salty, smoky flavor that is hard to match with anything else. We also add onion, salt, and freshly cracked pepper to give you a fresh-from-the-farmer's-kitchen flavor.

¼ pound sliced bacon

3 (15½-ounce) cans whole green beans (do not drain liquid)

¼ of a medium onion, minced

½ teaspoon salt

1 teaspoon sugar

½ teaspoon freshly ground black pepper

In a 2-quart saucepan on medium heat, cook the bacon until it is light brown but not crisp. When the bacon has browned, add the green beans along with their liquid. Add the salt, sugar, and pepper and mix well. Place the onion on top of the green beans, then cover the pan with a lid and bring the beans to a light boil. If the liquid in the pot is less than $1/3$ of the green beans, add enough water so the bottom third of the pan is both liquid and green beans. Turn the heat down to low and simmer the beans for 45 minutes to blend the flavors.

YIELD: 8 SERVINGS

CopyKat.com's **CRACKER BARREL OLD COUNTRY STORE®**

Mashed Potatoes

When I think of a Sunday dinner, I think of creamy mashed potatoes on my plate. Making mashed potatoes from scratch isn't hard to do, and once you try it you'll want to do it again and again.

6 medium russet potatoes	1 teaspoon salt
4 tablespoons margarine	½ teaspoon black pepper
¼ to ½ cup milk	

Bring a large pot of salted water to a boil. Wash the potatoes thoroughly, cut them into uniform 2-inch cubes, and drop them into the boiling water. Cook the potatoes until they are fork tender, then drain. Peel all but one of the potatoes. Place all the potatoes into a bowl with the margarine, milk, salt, and pepper and mash all the ingredients. I would not use an electric mixer for this; you do not want to take all of the lumps out. If you do use an electric mixer, just be careful not to totally mash the potatoes.

YIELD: 4 SERVINGS

CopyKat.com's **DAIRY QUEEN®**

Onion Rings

These are the onion rings that were found at a Dairy Queen® in East Texas many years ago. I know, because I made them myself during high school. I was amazed that at my first job I got to cook for real people. These onion rings are battered twice and then deep fried to lock in the tender onions on the inside, leaving you with a crisp outside.

4 cups vegetable oil
(or enough for your deep-fryer)

2 Vidalia onions

2 cups buttermilk

1 cup water

2 cups fine cracker crumbs

2 cups white cornmeal

2 cups flour

In a large pot or your deep-fryer, bring the oil up to 350°F. Slice the onions into ½-inch-thick rings, and set aside the very small rings for another use. In a large bowl, combine the buttermilk and water. In another bowl combine the cracker crumbs and cornmeal. One at a time, coat the onion rings with flour and then with the buttermilk mixture, and then coat them with the cornmeal mixture. Drop the rings into the hot oil and fry till golden, about 2 to 3 minutes. The onion rings are done when they float. Drain them on paper towels.

YIELD: 4 SERVINGS

Macaroni and Cheese

Maybe like you, I can't step into a cafeteria without macaroni and cheese appearing on my plate. Macaroni is creamy, cheesy, and tangy with the flavor of cheddar, and little else feels as good as a serving of this warm favorite. Luby's™ is one of those places that is just like stepping into Grandma's house, knowing you will be satisfied with the way that only your grandmother cooks.

2 cups (8 ounces)
dry elbow macaroni

2 tablespoons nonfat dry milk

2 tablespoons flour

1 tablespoon butter, melted

1¼ cups boiling water

3 cups (12 ounces) grated
American cheese, divided

¼ teaspoon salt

Cook the macaroni according to the package directions, then drain and set aside. Preheat the oven to 350°F. In a large bowl, mix the dry milk, flour, and butter. Gradually add the boiling water, beating constantly. Add about 1 cup cheese and continue beating until the sauce is smooth and creamy. Stir in the macaroni, 1 cup of the remaining cheese, and the salt. Transfer everything to a lightly greased 2-quart baking dish. Cover with foil and bake for 25 minutes. Remove the foil. Sprinkle the macaroni with the remaining cheese. Continue baking for 10 minutes, or until the cheese melts.

YIELD: 8 SERVINGS

CopyKat.com's **OUTBACK STEAKHOUSE™**

Mac-A-Roo 'N Cheese

Outback™ has macaroni and cheese only on their children's menu, but why should kids have all of the fun? I hate to say it, but when I order take out from Outback™, I add an order of their mac and cheese so I can have some at home.

> 2 cups dry penne pasta
>
> 8 ounces pasturized processed cheese (like Velveeta)
>
> ½ cup heavy cream

Cook the pasta according to the package directions. Cut the Velveeta into small cubes so it can melt easily. In a small saucepan, combine the cubed Velveeta and the heavy cream. Turn the heat on low and stir until all the cheese is melted. Reduce the heat to a simmer until you are ready to combine the cheese with the pasta. Once the pasta is done, drain it and pour it back into the pot where it was cooked. Add the cheese sauce and mix well.

   NOTE: If you need to reheat this later, the macaroni and cheese can be made creamy again by adding additional heavy cream. Honestly, you can use milk for this recipe, but the results are much better with the heavy cream. I have also had good results when I made this with a combination of half-and-half and whole milk.

YIELD: 4 SERVINGS

Sautéed Shrooms

★ ⏱

Sautéed mushrooms and steak go together like peanut butter and jelly. Sometimes you want these wonderfully seasoned mushrooms with an omelet or even on a baked potato. Unlike many recipes for sautéed mushrooms, these are primarily seasoned with wine and beef broth. The beefy flavor makes them taste so hearty that you will be thinking of more dishes to serve with these mushrooms.

1 (10½-ounce) can beef broth
½ cup diced yellow onions
2 (8-ounce) cans or jars small whole mushrooms (plus the juice of one can or jar)

⅓ cup Burgundy wine

Place the beef broth in a saucepan over medium heat. Add the onions and simmer 15 minutes. Add the mushrooms, mushroom juice, and wine and simmer for another 15 minutes.

YIELD: 4 SERVINGS

Frijoles a la Charra

Pappasito's™ is a chain of Tex-Mex restaurants in Texas, and this is one of my favorite recipes from there. In some circles these are known as drunken beans because the pinto beans are swimming in a flavorful, almost spicy broth. Now, these beans don't have to be served just as a side dish; they also make a great soup. They are light on the budget, but not light on taste. When serving them, you may want to sprinkle the top with chopped cilantro for a south-of-the-border flavor.

1½ pounds pinto beans, uncooked

1½ gallons (24 cups) cold water, divided

¾ pound bacon, chopped into 1-inch squares

½ cup plus 1 tablespoon finely chopped fresh garlic, divided

6 tablespoons finely chopped cilantro, divided

1 cup chopped white onions

1 tablespoon cumin

1 tablespoon chili powder

1½ tablespoons salt

2 cups chopped Roma tomatoes

Soak the pinto beans in 1 gallon cold water for 8 hours. Drain when ready to use. In a 2-gallon heavy pot over medium-high heat, cook the bacon pieces until well done (do not undercook the bacon). Add ½ cup garlic, 4 tablespoons chopped cilantro, and onions to the bacon. Cook until the onions are transparent, then add the soaked beans, cumin, and chili powder. Stir and add the remaining ½ gallon cold water. Turn the heat to medium-low. Add the salt and stir. Cook the beans slowly until they are fork tender, about 1 hour, stirring frequently to avoid burning the bottom. Add the tomatoes, the remaining tablespoon of garlic, and the remaining chopped cilantro, and serve.

YIELD: 12 SERVINGS

Sweet Carrot Pudding

Did you ever think people could clamor over carrots? They can and they will. This pudding may remind you of a sweet potato casserole. It is creamy and sweet, with a very smooth texture. No one will ever know that they are having carrots. Whenever I have made this recipe, the serving dish always comes back to the kitchen empty.

2 pounds (about 8 medium to large) carrots, peeled and cut into chunks

1 cup sugar

1½ teaspoons baking powder

1½ teaspoons vanilla

⅓ cup flour

½ teaspoon nutmeg

½ cup butter

4 eggs, beaten

1 to 2 tablespoons powdered sugar

Place the carrots in a medium pot and add enough water to cover them by an inch. Bring the water to a boil, and then reduce the heat down to a simmer for about 20 minutes or until the carrots are tender. Drain off the water and mash the carrots with a potato masher.

Preheat the oven to 350°F. In a large bowl, combine the mashed carrots, sugar, baking powder, vanilla, flour, nutmeg, and butter. Slowly drizzle the beaten eggs into the bowl. Mix together all the ingredients with an electric mixer for 2 minutes. Pour the mixture into a buttered 1½-quart casserole dish and bake it for approximately 1 hour, or until the casserole is well set. Once you remove the casserole from the oven, sprinkle powdered sugar over the top and serve.

YIELD: 8 SERVINGS

Cajun Rice ✓

Until I moved to the South, I never really knew what Cajun food was. A spicy delight, it has multiple layers of flavor with hints of heat. Please use a long-grain rice when making this dish. I did not like the results I got with Minute Rice®, but Success® Boil-in-Bag Rice did come out well.

1 pound lean ground beef

½ cup finely diced bell pepper

⅓ cup diced green onions

½ teaspoon garlic powder

½ teaspoon celery flakes

1 teaspoon Creole seasoning

¼ teaspoon crushed red pepper

4 cups cooked long grain rice, drained

¼ to ⅓ cup water

¼ teaspoon black pepper

In a frying pan on medium-high heat, stir together the ground beef and bell pepper and cook until beef loses its pink color and the bell pepper is soft. Remove any excess grease. Turn the temperature down to medium or medium-low. Add the green onions, garlic powder, celery flakes, Creole seasoning, crushed red pepper, cooked rice, water (you need to add enough water to make incorporating the spices easy; sometimes cooked rice can be a little dry), and pepper. Stir and cook everything until the ground beef is completely cooked and the liquid is gone, about 25 to 35 minutes. More Creole seasoning and red pepper may be added for the Cajun at heart.

YIELD: 8 SERVINGS

Red Beans

You can make it Mardi Gras any day with these beans, and here we use spices right out of your own kitchen cabinet to create the Cajun flavor. The ham hock in this recipe provides a wonderfully smoky flavor that infuses the beans. The lard is a key ingredient here, as this type of rendered fat gives the dish a lot of its Old South flavor. Lard is found in most grocery stores where solid shortening is sold.

3 (15½-ounce) cans red beans, divided

½ to ¾ pound smoked ham hock

1¼ cups water

½ teaspoon onion powder

½ teaspoon garlic salt

¼ teaspoon crushed red pepper

½ teaspoon salt, or to taste

¼ teaspoon freshly ground pepper

¼ cup plus 1 tablespoon lard

4 to 5 cups cooked long grain rice, drained

Pour 2 cans of beans with their liquid into a 2-quart pan. Add the smoked ham hock and water. Bring the pan to a simmer on medium heat for an hour, until the meat starts to loosen from the bone. Remove from the heat and cool until the ham hock is cool enough so the meat can be removed from the bone. Place the meat, beans, and liquid in a food processor. To the mixture add the onion powder, garlic salt, crushed red pepper, salt, pepper, and lard. Process for only 4 seconds. The beans should be chopped and have a soupy, liquid consistency. Now drain the liquid from the remaining can of beans and add the beans to the food processor. Process just for a second or two—you want these beans to remain almost whole. Pour the bean mixture back into the pan and cook slowly on low heat, stirring often, until ready to serve. Serve the beans over the cooked rice.

YIELD: 8 SERVINGS

Cheddar Bay Biscuits™

★ ⏱ 🫛

Can you even think of going to the Red Lobster® without having a biscuit or two? These biscuits are light and full of flavor. Garlic, Italian seasonings, and parsley make everyday biscuits into something very special. Want a light dinner? Why not make these and some soup? It's the perfect way to warm up on those cold nights.

2 cups Bisquick mix

½ cup cold water

¾ cup finely grated sharp cheddar cheese

¼ cup butter, melted

1 teaspoon parsley flakes

½ teaspoon garlic powder

½ teaspoon Italian seasoning

Preheat the oven to 450°F. Mix together the Bisquick, cold water, and cheese. Drop the biscuits onto a baking pan that has been sprayed with a nonstick baking spray. Mix together the melted butter, parsley flakes, garlic powder, and Italian seasoning and brush it on the biscuits. Bake for approximately 10 minutes.

YIELD: 12 BISCUITS

Foccacia

This is the foccacia that the Macaroni Grill™ used to make. What they serve now isn't as rustic as their older version. Thankfully, we put together this recipe long before they took the original off their menu. Semolina flour is a necessary ingredient in this recipe. You can find it in many grocery stores, either in the baking section or where the pasta is sold.

3 cups all-purpose flour	1½ cups hot milk (120 to 130°F)
¾ cup semolina flour	1 tablespoon fresh rosemary leaves
5 tablespoons olive oil, divided	
¼ teaspoon salt	1 teaspoon kosher salt
1 (¼-ounce) packet or 2¼ teaspoons quick-rising yeast	

Place the all-purpose flour and semolina flour, 2 tablespoons of the olive oil, the salt, and the yeast in the bowl of a mixer fitted with a dough hook. Blend the ingredients on medium speed. Reduce the speed to low and slowly drizzle the hot milk in. Raise the speed back to medium and continue mixing for 5 minutes.

Drizzle about 1 tablespoon of olive oil onto a cookie sheet. Remove the dough from the bowl, divide it in half, and shape it into two flat ovals. Cover the loaves with a towel and let them rest for 30 minutes. Preheat the oven to 400°F. Remove the towel and brush the dough with 1 to 2 tablespoons of the olive oil. Sprinkle ½ teaspoon of salt on each loaf, and sprinkle the rosemary evenly on top. Bake for approximately 20 minutes.

YIELD: 6 TO 8 SERVINGS

CopyKat.com's **SALTGRASS STEAK HOUSE™**

Garlic Mashed Potatoes

Garlic mashed potatoes like these are a decadent alternative to a baked potato at a steak house. A whole head of roasted garlic goes into these mashed potatoes, along with butter, freshly cracked pepper, and a touch of salt—and you don't even have to have a garlic roaster to make them.

5 medium russet potatoes, washed and scrubbed, skin on	1½ teaspoons olive oil
	½ teaspoon salt
5 tablespoons butter, softened, divided	½ teaspoon freshly ground black pepper
1 head garlic	½ to ¾ cup milk

Preheat the oven to 375°F. After washing the potatoes, rub them with 2 tablespoons of the softened butter and place them in the oven to bake until the potatoes are soft when checked with a fork, about a 60 to 75 minutes.

To prepare the garlic, cut the top off of the head of garlic so you can see the cloves without any peelings covering them. Spoon the vegetable oil on top of the garlic and wrap it in foil. Place it in the oven while the potatoes are baking. The garlic will take about 30 to 35 minutes to roast and should be soft and golden in color when it's done. Remove the garlic from the oven, let it cool slightly, and squeeze the soft garlic from about 4 or 5 cloves, depending on the size. You should end up with about 1½ teaspoons. More garlic may be added for the hearty.

When the potatoes are done, chop them into 1 to 2-inch cubes and place them in a large mixing bowl. Add the salt, the remaining 3 tablespoons of butter, pepper, and measured roasted garlic. Add ½ cup milk. Beat with an electric mixer until fluffy. There will be little chunks of potatoes that will not be completely mashed. The small lumps and peels will give these potatoes a hearty flavor. If the potatoes seem too dry, add a little more milk.

YIELD: 4 SERVINGS

Shiner Bock Beer Bread

As soon as you sit down at the Saltgrass Steak House™, your server will bring you a fresh, warm loaf of this bread. The malt of the beer gives this a unique flavor that you won't have in most freshly baked breads. Serve it with Saltgrass Steak House™ Honey Butter (page 250).

2¼ teaspoons (1 package) active dry yeast	2½ cups whole-wheat flour
¼ cup warm water (not hot)	½ teaspoon salt
¼ cup honey	¼ cup vegetable oil
1½ cups all-purpose flour	1½ to 1¾ cup Shiner Bock Beer, flat

In a large mixing bowl, dissolve the yeast with the warm water, then add the honey and stir. Let this mixture sit for approximately 5 minutes before using. If you are using quick-acting yeast instead of active dry, you can use this yeast mixture as soon as it is made. In a separate bowl, mix together the all-purpose flour, whole-wheat flour, and salt. Stir in the oil and slowly add the flat beer and the yeast mixture. Mix all the ingredients together. Place the dough on a floured surface and knead for at least 10 to 15 minutes. The dough may need a little more flour added to it if it sticks to your hands while you knead it. The finished dough will feel smooth and spongy and will not stick to your hands.

Place the dough in a lightly oiled bowl and cover it with plastic until it doubles in size, about 45 minutes (or sooner, if your kitchen is warmer). The dough should be left to rise at room temperature. Do not leave the dough in a drafty or overheated area.

When the dough has doubled, punch in the middle and let it rest for 5 minutes. Then divide the dough into four equal parts and shape them into round loaves. Place the loaves on a lightly oiled cookie sheet. With a knife, score the top of each loaf twice, 2 inches apart and about 2½ inches long. Cover the loaves loosely with plastic wrap until the loaves have doubled in size, about 45 minutes (again, depending upon the warmth of your kitchen).

Preheat the oven to 350°F and bake the loaves for about 30 minutes.

YIELD: 4 SMALL LOAVES

CopyKat.com's

Simple Beer Bread

Have you ever been to one of those wonderful parties where you can buy all sorts of tasty goodness in your home? They sell a mix for beer bread that tastes deliciously tangy and sweet. Here is my recreation of that recipe, and I think you will find that it tastes very close to that much more expensive mix.

3 cups self-rising flour

⅓ cup sugar

1 (12-ounce) beer (like Budweiser)

3 tablespoons butter, melted

Preheat the oven to 350°F. Spray a 9 x 5-inch loaf pan with nonstick spray. Combine the flour and sugar, then stir in the beer (you might have to use your hands to get it mixed thoroughly). The dough will be sticky. Pour the dough into the loaf pan and brush the top with the melted butter. Bake for 50 to 60 minutes, or until the top is golden brown. Allow the bread to cool slightly, then remove it from the pan to finish cooling.

YIELD: 1 LOAF, 12 SERVINGS

Onion Rings

★ 🫛

When I think about my time in high school and college, I can't help but think of Sonic®—circling the restaurant in my first car, seeing who else was there, and then biting into a crunchy and crisp onion ring. Sonic® is still around, more popular than ever, and making their onion rings fresh every day.

4 cups vegetable oil (or enough for your deep-fryer)	2 cups flour
	2 cups milk
2 Vidalia onions	2 cups white cornmeal
2 quarts (8 cups) ice water	

In a large pot or your deep-fryer, heat the oil to 350°F. Slice the onions into approximately 1-inch-thick rings. Place the onions into the ice water, separating out the rings when you put them into the bowl. Set the smaller rings aside for another use; it's easier to fry onion rings when they are all the same size. Take out the rings one at a time and coat them with flour, then gently dip them into a bowl of milk, and then coat them with cornmeal. Drop each one into the hot oil and fry till golden. Drain on paper towels. Enjoy!

YIELD: 4 SERVINGS

Desserts

XXXXXXXXXXXXXXXXXXXXXXXXXXXXXXXXXXXX

O ften when dining out you may not have
any room left for dessert, but I'll show
you how to make those classic restaurant-style
desserts in your own kitchen so you don't
have to miss out. And you don't have to serve
desserts after dinner only. They're wonderful
dishes to bring to new neighbors or over to
friends' homes.

I have included a wide variety of desserts
in this chapter. You will see ice cream pies,
cheesecakes, candies, brownies, and more.
A lot of people say baking is really hard, or
overly complicated, but it really isn't. You
simply need to follow directions and measure
precisely. Take a couple of moments when you
are ready to start the recipe and check to see
that you have all the ingredients. If you don't,
I don't recommend making substitutions like
you would in cooking a soup—precision is key
when it comes to baking. So if you haven't tried
baking, give it a chance, and you may discover
you have a baker inside of you after all.

CopyKat.com's **BASKIN-ROBBINS®**

Turtle Pie

No need to pay the high prices in an ice cream store—you can make this easy ice cream pie at home. This is a nice way to surprise your guests with a little something out of the ordinary. You don't need to limit yourself to just the flavors listed here. Consider using chocolate and peanut butter ice cream garnished with a couple of crushed peanut butter cups on top.

1 quart pralines-and-cream ice cream	½ cup hot fudge sauce
1 prepared chocolate cookie crumb pie crust	1 cup caramel sauce
	1 cup pecan pieces

Allow the ice cream to sit at room temperature long enough to soften, but do not let it melt! Line the bottom of the pie crust with the hot fudge sauce. Spread the ice cream into the crust. Top it with the caramel sauce and pecans. If you want an extra-rich flavor, cook the pecans in a couple of tablespoons of real butter until they become aromatic and roast just a bit before you put them on the pie. Put the pie back in the freezer until it becomes solid again.

YIELD: 8 SERVINGS

Bananas Foster

★ ♟ ♥

Bananas Foster was originally created by Brennan's™, and it is hard to make this recipe any better. Butter, caramelized bananas, cinnamon, nutmeg, and different liqueurs make it a true delight. Don't let igniting the banana mixture stop you from making this dish. This is one of my favorite desserts to make when company comes over because it is very inexpensive, and the flavor payoff is incredible.

¼ cup butter

1 cup brown sugar

½ teaspoon cinnamon

4 bananas, cut in half and then sliced in half lengthwise

¼ cup banana liqueur

¼ cup dark rum
spiced rum also works well)

4 scoops vanilla ice cream

Combine the butter, brown sugar, and cinnamon in a large skillet over low heat. Cook, stirring, until the sugar dissolves completely. Place the banana pieces into the pan, and cook until they start to turn brown. Add in the banana liqueur and dark rum. Cook the mixture for about a minute before you ignite it. If you have a gas stove, you can ignite the mixture by tilting the pan slightly so it just catches the flame. If you have an electric stove, you can very carefully light the mixture with a match or a long-stemmed lighter. You can even sprinkle some cinnamon over the flame to entertain your guests. Wait until the flames subside, and then spoon the bananas over the ice cream and pour the sauce on top.

YIELD: 2 SERVINGS

Cheesecake

The Cheesecake Factory's® signature dish is, of course, their cheesecake, and they also make high-end frozen cheesecakes that are available in many wholesale clubs. I thought this cake in particular was delicious and unique. The crust has a variety of nuts that add a nice flavor to the filling.

CRUST:
¼ cup finely chopped pecans
¼ cup finely chopped almonds
¼ cup finely chopped walnuts
¾ cup finely chopped vanilla wafers
2 tablespoons melted butter

FILLING:
3 (8-ounce) packages cream cheese
1⅓ cups sugar
5 large eggs
¼ cup flour
2 teaspoons vanilla extract
2 teaspoons lemon juice
1 pound (16 ounces) sour cream

FOR CRUST: Mix the pecans, almonds, walnuts, and vanilla wafer crumbs with the melted butter. Press the mixture into a lightly buttered 9-inch springform pan, trying to line the sides as much as possible, about 1½-inches up the sides of the pan. Set aside.

FOR FILLING: For the best results, let all of your ingredients reach room temperature before you begin preparing your cheesecake filling.

Keep the mixer on a low setting during the beating and mixing process. With an electric mixer, beat the cream cheese until it's light and fluffy, approximately 2 to 3 minutes. Add the sugar a little at a time and continue beating until creamy. Add the eggs one at a time and beat after each egg. When the eggs have been mixed into the cream cheese, add the flour, vanilla, and lemon juice and mix well. Add the sour cream last and beat well.

FOR ASSEMBLY: Preheat the oven to 325°F. Pour the filling into the crust. Place the cheesecake on the top rack in the middle of the oven and bake for

1 hour and 15 minutes. When the time is up, turn off the oven and prop open the oven door. Leave the cheesecake in the oven for 1 hour, then remove it. Let it cool at room temperature, then test the cheesecake by touching it with your fingertips—there should be no heat coming from it. When it's cool enough, put the cheesecake in the refrigerator for 24 hours. The wait is worth it. The flavor ripens and becomes enriched.

YIELD: 16 SERVINGS

Oreo® Cheesecake

Who can turn down cheesecake with Oreo® cookies? Cheesecake is rich and luscious on its own, but adding Oreos® takes it to another level. The Oreos'® dark chocolate cookie and creamy center really add a lot of flavor.

CRUST:
1½ cups Oreo cookie crumbs (about 23 Oreo cookies)
2 tablespoons melted butter

FILLING:
3 (8-ounce) packages cream cheese
1 cup sugar
5 large eggs
2 teaspoons vanilla extract
¼ teaspoon salt
¼ cup flour
½ pound (8 ounces) sour cream
15 Oreo cookies, coarsely chopped, divided

FOR CRUST: Mix the Oreo cookie crumbs with the melted butter. Press the cookie crumbs into a lightly buttered 9-inch springform pan, covering the bottom and 1½-inches up the sides with crumbs. Set aside.

FOR FILLING: For the best results, let all of your ingredients reach room temperature before you begin preparing your cheesecake filling.

Keep the mixer on a low setting during the mixing and beating process. With an electric mixer, beat the cream cheese it's until light and fluffy. Add the sugar gradually and continue beating until well mixed. Add the eggs one at a time and continue to beat until blended. Add the vanilla, salt, and flour to the mixer and beat until smooth. Add the sour cream and beat well. Turn off the mixer and stir in about 6 coarsely chopped Oreo cookies with a spoon.

FOR ASSEMBLY: Preheat the oven to 325°F. Pour the filling into the crust and place the remaining coarsely chopped Oreo cookies on top. Place the cheesecake in the middle of the top rack of the oven and bake for 1 hour and 15 minutes. When the time is up, turn off the oven and prop open the oven door. Leave the cheesecake in the oven for 1 hour. Remove it from the oven and let it cool at room temperature, then test the cheesecake by touching it with your fingertips—there should be no heat coming from it. When it's cool enough, put the cheesecake in the refrigerator for 24 hours. It is worth the anticipation. Just like in a stew or chili, the flavors are much better the second day.

YIELD: 16 SERVINGS

Chocolate Brownie Sundae ✓

Chili's® knows how to turn an ordinary brownie into something that is almost an event in itself. This is a delightful treat, and it's a great way to pump up a brownie mix. These brownies are packed with walnuts, and then we add ice cream, hot fudge topping, and more—perfect for chocolate lovers.

1 (15-ounce) package fudge chocolate brownie mix

1 (14-ounce) package walnuts, coarsely chopped, divided

vanilla ice cream

1 (16-ounce) jar chocolate fudge topping

1 (12-ounce) jar maraschino cherries

Preheat the oven to the temperature indicated on the package of the brownie mix. Follow the directions on the package for fudge-style brownies. Add 1½ cups coarsely chopped walnuts to the batter and stir. Pour the batter into a 9 x 13-inch pan so the brownies will not be too thick. Bake according to the package directions, but do not overbake. Personally, I like to leave the brownies just a little gooey.

To assemble individual servings, place a large round spoonful of vanilla ice cream on top of a 4 x 4-inch slice of brownie. Cover it with fudge, sprinkle about a tablespoon of walnuts on top, and add a maraschino cherry!

YIELD: 6 SERVINGS

Mighty High Ice Cream Pie

While this recipe was being developed, I hate to say how many pieces of this pie the testers ate. You are unlikely to have it around for any length of time—it's that good. For serving, the pie looks nice if you drizzle caramel and chocolate on the plate and then place a slice of pie on top.

1 premade Oreo cookie crust

1 (6-ounce) package Heath bits

1 cup semisweet chocolate chips

½ gallon vanilla ice cream

1 (16-ounce) jar chocolate fudge topping

1 (16-ounce) jar caramel topping

The real secret to this recipe is keeping everything as cold as possible. Start the recipe the night before by placing the pie crust, Heath bits, and chocolate chips in the freezer. The next day, finely chop the frozen Heath bits in a food processor, then, in a separate batch, finely chop the frozen chocolate chips. Put the pieces back in the freezer. Soften the ice cream just until it's workable (so bits of topping can be stirred into the ice cream without it melting). Place the softened ice cream in a chilled mixing bowl and add the ground Heath bits and chocolate chips. Stir and mix well. Spread the ice cream in the frozen pie shell and refreeze it for about 4 hours, or until it's frozen hard. Microwave $1/3$ cup of the chocolate fudge topping so that it melts and makes a stream when it's poured from a measuring cup or spoon. The caramel may make a stream without being heated, but if it doesn't, slightly heat it like the chocolate topping. Remove the pie from the freezer and stream the chocolate and caramel sauce on top of the pie. Place it back in the freezer. When it's completely frozen, cover the pie tightly and it will keep in the freezer for several days.

YIELD: 8 SERVINGS

CopyKat.com's CICI'S™

Cherry Dessert Pizza

No one makes dessert pizza like CiCi's™, and canned cherry pie filling helps you make this wonderful fruit pizza. Serve as a dessert or a wonderful afterschool snack for the gang.

CRUMB TOPPING:
½ cup flour

3 tablespoons sugar

1 tablespoon brown sugar

⅛ teaspoon salt

¼ cup butter, softened

PIZZA:
1 (1-pound) package pizza dough mix

1 (20-ounce) can cherry pie filling

FOR CRUMB TOPPING: In a small bowl, mix together the flour, sugar, brown sugar, and salt. Add the butter to the mixture and blend until the topping resembles cornmeal. This topping can also be used on baked fruit deserts, like a crumble or a crisp. Set aside.

FOR PIZZA: Preheat the oven to 450°F. Prepare the pizza dough as directed on the package. Spread the dough on a greased 12-inch pizza pan and prick it with a fork 8 to 10 times. Place the pizza dough in the oven for 5 minutes, then remove it from the oven and spread the cherry pie filling on top, leaving an edge for a crust so your fingers stay clean when you munch on this pizza. Sprinkle on ¼ cup of the crumb topping and place the pizza back into the oven and bake for 20 to 25 minutes, or until the dough is golden brown.

YIELD: 8 SERVINGS

CopyKat.com's CICI'S™

Chocolate Dessert Pizza

With chocolate pudding and pizza dough, you can turn a couple of basic ingredients into something really special.

CRUMB TOPPING:
½ cup flour

3 tablespoons sugar

1 tablespoon brown sugar

⅛ teaspoon salt

¼ cup butter, softened

PIZZA:
1 (1-pound) package pizza dough mix

1 (3.4-ounce) box chocolate pudding mix (not instant)

FOR CRUMB TOPPING: In a small bowl, mix together the flour, sugar, brown sugar, and salt. Add the butter to the mixture and blend until the topping resembles cornmeal. Set aside.

FOR PIZZA: Prepare the pudding according to the package directions and allow it to cool. Preheat the oven to 450°F. Prepare the pizza dough as directed on the package. Spread the dough on a greased 12-inch pizza pan and prick it with a fork 8 to 10 times. Place the pizza dough in the oven for 5 minutes. Remove it from oven and spread ¾ cup of chocolate pudding on the dough, leaving a small crust around the edges. Then sprinkle on ¼ cup of crumb topping. Place the pizza back in the oven and bake for 18 to 20 minutes, until the crumb topping is a little crisp.

YIELD: 8 SERVINGS

Funnel Cakes

★

I've had so many requests for funnel cake recipes over the years, and here is one that will make you think you are at the county fair. Best of all, you can serve them however you like. We have seen these with powdered sugar, chocolate sauce, strawberry topping, whipped cream, and a few other goodies. They will certainly cost less than the five-dollar price tag at the fair!

10 cups vegetable oil, for deep-frying

2 eggs, lightly beaten

1½ cups milk

¼ cup brown sugar, packed

2 cups flour

1½ teaspoons baking powder

¼ teaspoon salt

confectioners' sugar, for dusting

In an electric skillet or deep-fryer, heat the oil to 375°F. In a bowl, combine the eggs, milk, and brown sugar. In a separate bowl, combine the flour, baking powder, and salt. Beat the flour mixture into the egg mixture with a whisk until smooth. There are two methods of pouring the batter into the oil: the first, and best, method is to use a funnel, but if you don't have a funnel, the batter can be poured from a liquid measuring cup. Cover the bottom of a funnel spout with your finger; ladle ½ cup batter into the funnel. Holding the funnel several inches above the hot oil, take your finger off the spout and move the funnel in a spiral motion until all of the batter is released, scraping the funnel with a rubber spatula if needed. Fry the dough for 2 minutes on each side, or until golden brown. Drain on paper towels. Repeat with the remaining batter. Dust the funnel cakes with confectioners' sugar and serve warm.

YIELD: 6 TO 8 FUNNEL CAKES

Carrot Cake

★

Who makes a carrot cake better than your grandma? That would be Cracker Barrel®, where we all love to shop and eat. This carrot cake is packed full of grated carrots, nuts, pineapple, and more. Since it isn't a layer cake, it is easy to put together. Best of all, it gets topped with a rich and creamy cream cheese frosting.

CAKE:
3 cups flour
2 teaspoons baking powder
2 teaspoons baking soda
½ teaspoon salt
2 teaspoons ground cinnamon
1 teaspoon ground nutmeg
½ teaspoon ground cloves
1¼ cups vegetable oil
1½ cups sugar
½ cup brown sugar
2 teaspoons vanilla extract
3 eggs
1 cup crushed pineapple
(8-ounce can, with juice)
¾ cup finely chopped walnuts
½ cup finely shredded coconut
2 cups finely shredded carrots
½ cup raisins, soaked in water
until plump, then drained

CREAM CHEESE FROSTING:
1 (8-ounce) package
cream cheese
½ cup butter, at room
temperature
1 teaspoon vanilla extract
2 cups powdered sugar
½ cup chopped pecans,
for garnish

FOR CAKE: Preheat the oven to 350°F and grease and flour a 9 x 13-inch pan. Mix together the flour, baking powder, baking soda, salt, cinnamon, nutmeg, and cloves. Set aside. In a large bowl with an electric mixer, mix the oil, sugar, brown sugar, vanilla, and eggs until smooth and fluffy. Add the pineapple, walnuts, coconut, carrots, and raisins and blend well. Gradually add the flour mixture in two parts, mixing until blended thoroughly.

Pour the batter into the prepared pan and bake for about 40 to 50 minutes, or until a toothpick inserted into the cake comes out clean. When the cake is cool, frost it with the Cream Cheese Frosting.

FOR CREAM CHEESE FROSTING: With an electric mixer, blend the cream cheese and butter until light and fluffy. Add the vanilla, then add the powdered sugar a little at a time until all has been blended well. Turn the mixer on high and beat until the frosting is light and fluffy. Spread the frosting over the cooled cake and sprinkle pecans over the top.

YIELD: 24 SERVINGS

Cherry Chocolate Cobbler

★

This is a seasonal favorite from the Cracker Barrel®, but you can enjoy this rich chocolate goodness anytime. Be sure to serve this with premium vanilla bean ice cream.

1½ cups all-purpose flour

½ cup granulated sugar

2 teaspoons baking powder

½ teaspoon salt

¼ cup butter

1 (6-ounce) package semisweet chocolate chips

¼ cup milk

1 egg, slightly beaten

1 (21-ounce) can cherry pie filling

½ cup finely chopped nuts (both walnuts and pecans can be used)

Preheat the oven to 350°F. In a large mixing bowl, combine the flour, sugar, baking powder, salt, and butter. Cut the mixture with a pastry blender until the crumbs are the size of small peas. In a double boiler over hot (not boiling) water, melt the chocolate chips. Allow the chocolate to cool 5 minutes at room temperature. Add the milk and egg to the chocolate mixture; mix well. Blend the chocolate into the flour and butter mixture; mix well. Spread the cherry pie filling in the bottom of a 2-quart casserole. Drop the chocolate batter randomly over the cherries. Sprinkle nuts all over the top. Bake 40 to 45 minutes; you know this is done when you gently shake the pan and the cobbler does not give.

YIELD: 8 SERVINGS

Coca-Cola® Cake

★

Sometimes some recipes use really unusual ingredients. Would you think that Coca-Cola® and chocolate would go together so well? This wonderful cake isn't always on the menu at Cracker Barrel®; it's one of their seasonal items. With this recipe, you don't have to guess when they'll have it, and you can make it any time you want.

CAKE:
½ cup butter

1 cup Coca-Cola

1 square (1 ounce) semisweet baking chocolate

¾ cup miniature marshmallows

½ cup shortening

½ cup vegetable oil

2 teaspoons vanilla extract

2 cups sugar

2 eggs

¾ cup buttermilk

2⅓ cups flour

1 teaspoon baking soda

¾ cup cocoa powder

1½ teaspoons baking powder

½ teaspoon salt

FROSTING:
½ cup butter

½ cup cocoa powder

1 teaspoon vanilla extract

¼ cup chocolate syrup

¼ cup Coca-Cola

3 cups powdered sugar

FOR CAKE: Preheat the oven to 350°F and grease and flour a 9 x 13-inch baking pan. In a saucepan, combine the butter, Coca-Cola, and the semisweet baking chocolate. Bring the mixture to a boil, then remove the pan from the heat. Add the marshmallows and stir until everything is blended and the marshmallows dissolve. Set aside to cool to room temperature.

In a large mixing bowl, use an electric mixer to blend the shortening, vegetable oil, vanilla, and sugar until fluffy. Add the eggs and buttermilk and beat until smooth. In a separate bowl, mix together the flour, baking soda, cocoa powder, baking powder, and salt. Add half the flour mixture to the wet ingredients and beat well. Scrape the bowl from time to time to clean the sides off so the ingredients are incorporated into the batter. Add the cooled Coca-Cola mixture and beat well. Add the remaining flour mixture and beat until the batter is completely smooth, about 3 to 4 minutes. The batter will be thick. Scrape the batter into the prepared baking pan, and bake on the top rack of the oven for 35 to 40 minutes, until a toothpick inserted into the middle of the cake comes out clean. While the cake is baking, prepare the frosting.

FOR FROSTING: In a mixing bowl, cream the butter until light and fluffy, then add the cocoa powder, vanilla, chocolate syrup, and Coca-Cola and beat until smooth. Add the powdered sugar a little at a time, beating constantly. Scrape the sides of the bowl from time to time to get all ingredients into the frosting. If the frosting seems a little dry, add 2 to 3 tablespoons more Coca-Cola and beat well.

FOR ASSEMBLY: Frost the cake when it's warm. Serve with natural vanilla bean ice cream and enjoy.

YIELD: 24 SERVINGS

Strawberry Shortcake

Go back in time with an old-fashioned treat. The recipe isn't a secret, and there are two ways to make this tasty summertime dessert: You can use the quick-and-easy method, using frozen or premade pound cake and frozen strawberries, or you can make everything from scratch. While the Cracker Barrel® uses frozen strawberries, I really like fresh much more. I think you can jazz up this recipe by using fresh strawberries, fresh whipped cream, and if you are up for it, a homemade pound cake, like Sara Lee® Pound Cake (page 207).

1 homemade pound cake or 1 frozen or premade pound cake	1 tablespoon superfine sugar (optional)
1 pound fresh strawberries or 1 pint frozen, sweetened strawberries, thawed	1 pint heavy whipping cream or 1 can (7 ounces) whipped cream
vanilla extract (optional)	4 scoops premium vanilla ice cream

Prepare the homemade pound cake, if using. If you're using fresh strawberries, prepare them several hours ahead of time by cleaning and slicing them. Place them in a bowl with the superfine sugar, if available, and mix well. Chill them in the refrigerator until ready to serve. If you're using fresh whipped cream, you may want to add a touch of vanilla extract for some extra flavor along with 2 teaspoons of sugar, then whip the cream with an electric mixer until firm.

Cut two 1-inch slices of the pound cake and slice them in half. In a large bowl place the four pieces of pound cake across from each other, so the ice cream will be surrounded by the pound cake. Spoon the prepared fresh strawberries or thawed frozen strawberries onto the cake; add one scoop of vanilla ice cream to each slice, and then top with whipped cream.

YIELD: 4 SERVINGS

Cinna Stix®

These are wonderful to make for a stay-at-home pizza night or for when you want a little snack. They are easy to make, and you can save money by making them at home.

STICKS:
1 (16-ounce) package pizza dough mix, or your favorite recipe

½ cup sugar

2 teaspoons cinnamon

¼ cup melted butter, divided

ICING:
1 pound (3½ cups) powdered sugar

½ teaspoon vanilla extract

1 tablespoon milk

1 tablespoon melted butter

FOR STICKS: Preheat the oven to 350°F. Roll out the pizza dough into a 10 x 12-inch rectangle. Cut the rectangle in half across the longest side, and then cut the other direction into eighths. You should have 16 individual pieces now. Combine the sugar and cinnamon in a bowl and mix well. Brush the dough with half of the melted butter and sprinkle half of the cinnamon-sugar mix on top of the "stix." Place the pieces on a lightly greased baking sheet and bake for approximately 15 minutes.

FOR ICING: While the sticks are baking, make the icing by combining the powdered sugar, vanilla, milk, and butter. You may need to add additional milk to thin down the icing.

FOR ASSEMBLY: When the "stix" come out of the oven, brush them with any butter that you may have left and sprinkle with the rest of the cinnamon-sugar mixture. Serve the "stix" with the icing.

YIELD: 16 "STIX"

Bread Pudding

They make delicious bread at the Golden Corral®, so why would their bread pudding be any different? Melted butter, milk, spices, and day-old bread make a creamy and filling dessert.

BREAD PUDDING:
2 cups whole milk

½ cup melted butter

¼ teaspoon salt

2 eggs

⅓ cup dark brown sugar

1 teaspoon cinnamon

3 cups cubed French bread, partially dried

VANILLA SAUCE:
1 cup whole milk

2 tablespoons butter

½ cup granulated sugar

1 teaspoon vanilla extract

1 tablespoon flour

dash of salt

FOR BREAD PUDDING: Preheat the oven to 350°F and oil an 8 x 11-inch pan well. In a large saucepan, heat the milk, butter, and salt together, and remove the pan from the heat when the butter is completely melted; do not let the milk boil. In a separate bowl with an electric mixer, beat the eggs, then add brown sugar and cinnamon. Add the egg mixture to the saucepan with the hot melted butter and milk, stirring rapidly to make sure that the eggs don't cook into solid pieces. Carefully stir in the bread cubes; do not beat. Transfer the bread pudding to the prepared pan and bake for about 40 minutes, until a toothpick inserted in the center comes out clean. Set aside.

FOR VANILLA SAUCE: In a saucepan, combine the milk, butter, sugar, vanilla, flour, and salt together and bring to a boil for 3 to 4 minutes, stirring constantly. Remove the pan from the heat and set it aside for 5 minutes. Pour about half the sauce on the warm bread pudding and pour the remainder in a serving bowl for those who desire that little extra. This pudding is best served warm, but is also great at room temperature.

YIELD: 18 SERVINGS

CopyKat.com's **HOUSTON'S™**

Walnut Apple Cobbler

★

When I tried this one at Houston's™, I knew I had to re-create the recipe. This is a most delicious apple cobbler, and I combine many different layers of apple flavor to make it taste just right. It's really best when served warm.

FILLING:

1 (20-ounce) can sliced apples (see note)

2 cups coarsely chopped walnuts

1 tablespoon plus 2 teaspoons cinnamon

1/8 teaspoon nutmeg

1/8 teaspoon salt

3 tablespoons melted butter

1/4 cup light corn syrup

1 cup brown sugar

COOKIE TOPPING:

1/2 cup butter, chilled

1/2 cup brown sugar

1/4 teaspoon vanilla extract

1 egg yolk

1/2 cup flour

1/4 teaspoon baking powder

1/4 teaspoon salt

FOR FILLING: Reserve 1½ cups apple juice and 1 cup drained apples from the can. In a mixing bowl, combine the apple juice, drained apples, walnuts, cinnamon, nutmeg, salt, butter, corn syrup, and brown sugar and stir well. Set aside.

FOR COOKIE TOPPING: This is easy to blend in a food processor. Cut the butter into four pieces and add them to the food processor with the brown sugar, vanilla, and egg yolk. Process until blended. Add the flour, baking powder, and salt, and blend until the dry ingredients are well mixed. A ball of dough should form very quickly. Remove the dough from the processor, place it between two pieces of waxed paper, and chill it just long enough so it can be rolled out without sticking to the waxed paper.

FOR ASSEMBLY: Preheat the oven to 375°F. Spray an 8 x 11½-inch baking pan with nonstick spray and pour in the walnut filling. Roll out the cookie dough topping so it's the same size as the pan, and cover the filling with it. Bake for 20 to 24 minutes until the top is golden brown. The cobbler should be served hot with the crust side down and a generous serving of your favorite vanilla ice cream on top.

NOTE: For this recipe, you divide the can of apples into the apples and the juice. You will have some apples left over. Depending on the brand, you may need to add some more apple juice, or you can add a little water to make up the difference.

YIELD: 10 SERVINGS

CopyKat.com's **KEEBLER®**

Almond Shortbread Cookies

It's hard to beat almond shortbread cookies. You can serve them freshly baked and warm, and they'll taste like the Keebler® elves have been busy in your kitchen. I found that using the product Butter Buds®, a powdered butter flavoring, is a great way to add butter flavor to the cookies.

1¾ cups flour	1 egg, beaten
½ teaspoon cream of tartar	1 teaspoon vanilla extract
1½ teaspoons baking soda	2 teaspoons almond extract
½ cup butter, softened	¼ teaspoon Butter Buds
½ cup sugar	¼ teaspoon salt
½ cup powdered sugar	½ cup finely chopped almonds

Mix together the flour, cream of tartar, and baking soda and set aside. In a mixing bowl, beat the butter, sugar, and powdered sugar together with an electric mixer until fluffy. Add the beaten egg, vanilla, almond extract, Butter Buds, and salt. Beat all the ingredients until well blended. Add the flour mixture about a third at a time and beat until smooth. The dough will come away from the sides of the mixing bowl and will look a little dry. When the cookie dough is blended, stir in the almonds with a spoon. Cover the bowl with plastic wrap and chill the dough for 30 to 45 minutes.

　　Preheat the oven to 350°F. Roll the chilled cookie dough into 1 to 1¼-inch balls and place the balls on an ungreased cookie sheet approximately 1 inch apart. Flatten the balls until they are about ¼-inch thick. Bake the cookies for about 12 to 15 minutes until slightly golden. Remove the cookies from the cookie sheet and place them on paper towels to cool.

YIELD: APPROXIMATELY 2½ DOZEN COOKIES

CopyKat.com's **KEEBLER®**

Pecan Sandies

Shortbread cookies are delightful, and since we shared our recipe for Keebler's® almond cookies, we couldn't stop there. These pecan sandies aren't to be missed. These go so well with a cup of coffee or when you want just a little bit of sweetness.

1¾ cups flour	½ cup powdered sugar
½ teaspoon cream of tartar	1 teaspoon vanilla extract
½ teaspoon baking soda	¼ teaspoon salt
½ cup vegetable shortening	1 egg, beaten
½ cup sugar	½ cup finely chopped pecans

Mix together the flour, cream of tartar, and baking soda and set aside. In a mixing bowl, beat together the vegetable shortening, sugar, and powdered sugar with an electric mixer until fluffy. Add the vanilla, salt, and egg and beat until smooth. Add the flour mixture to the wet ingredients about a third at time. Beat until completely mixed through. The dough will seem a little thick. Stir the pecans into the cookie dough with a spoon and blend well. Cover the bowl with plastic wrap and chill the dough for 30 to 45 minutes. This helps the cookies spread less on the baking sheet when they're in the oven.

Preheat the oven to 350°F. Roll the cookie dough into 1 to 1¼-inch balls and place them on an ungreased cookie sheet about 1 inch apart. Flatten the balls to about ¼-inch thick. Bake for 12 to 15 minutes until they are slightly golden.

YIELD: APPROXIMATELY 2½ DOZEN COOKIES

CopyKat.com's **KOZY SHACK®**

Rice Pudding

You can make homemade puddings that are so much better than any instant package, and this creamy and sweet rice pudding is easy to make. It has a delightful vanilla flavor, and best of all, you can keep this one in your refrigerator for a few days, unlike instant puddings. This is a wonderful way to make a dessert when you want something light and you don't have a ton of ingredients in your pantry. This recipe can easily be made with what you're likely to have on hand.

¾ cup sugar

⅓ cup flour

¼ teaspoon salt

2 cups whole milk

3 egg yolks

1 cup cooked long grain rice (water-polished rice, if available)

½ teaspoon vanilla extract

Place the sugar, flour, salt, and milk in a saucepan over medium-low heat, and stir until the mixture begins to boil. Let it boil while stirring constantly for 2 to 3 minutes. Remove the pan from the heat. Beat the egg yolks together in a separate bowl and add ½ cup of the hot milk mixture into the egg yolks and mix well. Pour the egg yolks and the rice into the hot milk mixture and place the pan back on the stove. Continue to cook for 2 to 3 minutes. Stir constantly so that no lumps of pudding stick to the bottom of the pan. Remove the pan from the heat, add the vanilla, and blend well. Chill before serving. Add your favorite garnish. Fruit, whipped topping, or a little cinnamon are nice.

YIELD: 4 SERVINGS

CopyKat.com's **LA MADELEINE™**

Strawberries Romanoff

★ 🎩 ⏱

This is always my most-ordered menu item at La Madeleine™. These strawberries make an elegant dessert or are wonderful to serve at a brunch for guests. You can also use the creamy sauce on other kinds of fruit. I like to use blueberries and cantaloupe when I have them on hand. The brandy-infused sauce will keep well in your refrigerator for several days.

1 pound (2 pints) strawberries	2 tablespoons brown sugar
1 cup heavy whipping cream	4 tablespoons brandy
½ cup sour cream	

Cut the tops off the strawberries and be sure they are dry. Mix together the heavy whipping cream, sour cream, brown sugar, and the brandy. Beat with an electric mixer until the sauce becomes thick. Place the strawberries into glasses and spoon the sauce on top.

YIELD: 4 SERVINGS

CopyKat.com's LUBY'S™

Coconut Cream Pie

This pie is a classic that will remind you of being at your grandmother's house a long time ago.

FILLING:
5 cups half-and-half
¼ cup (½ stick) butter
1 cup sugar
3 extra-large eggs
¼ cup cornstarch
1 teaspoon vanilla extract
¼ teaspoon salt
1 cup miniature marshmallows
1 cup flaked coconut, divided
2 prebaked 9-inch pie shells
(see note)

MERINGUE:
1¼ cups egg whites (from 8 to 9 extra-large eggs)
1 teaspoon cream of tartar
1½ cups sugar

FOR FILLING: Combine the half-and-half and butter in a saucepan. Bring the mixture just to a boil over medium heat. In a medium bowl, whisk together the sugar, eggs, cornstarch, vanilla, and salt until the cornstarch is completely dissolved and the mixture is well blended. Gradually add the sugar mixture to the half-and-half mixture in the saucepan, stirring constantly with a wire whisk. Cook, stirring constantly, about 1 minute, or until thickened. Add the marshmallows and ¾ cup of the coconut. Cook and stir until the marshmallows melt and the filling is well blended. Pour the filling into the prepared pie shells. Refrigerate at least 2 hours.

FOR MERINGUE: In a large bowl, beat the egg whites and cream of tartar until soft peaks form. Add the sugar a small amount at a time, beating constantly until stiff peaks form.

FOR ASSEMBLY: Spread half the meringue over each pie to the edge of the crust. Sprinkle each pie with ¼ cup of the remaining coconut. Preheat the oven to 350° degrees. Bake the pies for 12 to 15 minutes, or until lightly browned. Refrigerate until served.

NOTE: Pie shells can be purchased frozen and then baked according to the package directions, or you may want to bake your own from your personal favorite recipe.

<><><><><><><><><><><><><><><><><><><><>

YIELD: 8 SERVINGS

Brownie Cheesecake Cups

Mall food—food that is found primarily in shopping malls—is an interesting dining category in itself, and it's one of my favorites. These brownies are chocolatey and are filled with a tangy cream cheese filling.

FILLING:

3 tablespoons butter, softened

2 (3-ounce) packages cream cheese, softened

$\frac{1}{3}$ cup sugar

2 tablespoons flour

1 teaspoon vanilla extract

BROWNIES:

2 cups sugar

$1\frac{1}{4}$ cups flour

$\frac{1}{4}$ teaspoon salt

6 tablespoons cocoa powder

4 eggs, beaten

$\frac{3}{4}$ cup vegetable oil

1 teaspoon vanilla extract

FOR FILLING: Mix the butter, cream cheese, sugar, flour, and vanilla together with an electric mixer and blend well. Set aside.

FOR BROWNIES: Mix the sugar, flour, salt, cocoa powder, eggs, oil, and vanilla together with an electric mixer until smooth.

FOR ASSEMBLY: Preheat the oven to 350°F and line a cupcake pan with paper cupcake cups. Reserve ½ cup of the brownie batter for topping the cream cheese mixture. Fill the cupcake cups half full with the brownie batter, then spoon the cream cheese filling on top of the brownie batter until the cups are three-quarters full. Top each one with a scant teaspoon of the reserved brownie batter. Bake for 20 to 25 minutes, or until the cheesecake cups no longer shake in the pan—but a little jiggle is okay, and sometimes I prefer to leave these a little underbaked.

YIELD: APPROXIMATELY 1 DOZEN

Decadent Walnut Chocolate Fudge

★

This tasty treat features a soft texture and a complex chocolate flavor. Fudge can be made at home, but it takes a little more attention than some other dishes. As long as you measure the ingredients carefully and follow the directions, you'll turn out fudge just like the professionals. Your friends will gladly assist in tasting your creations.

2 cups sugar

¾ cup evaporated milk

½ cup light corn syrup

¼ teaspoon salt

2 tablespoons butter

1 cup semisweet chocolate chips

1 cup milk chocolate chips

1 teaspoon vanilla extract

1⅓ cups miniature marshmallows

1 cup chopped walnuts or small walnut pieces

Spray a 2-quart saucepan with nonstick spray and combine the sugar, evaporated milk, corn syrup, salt, and butter in the pan. Place the pan on medium heat and stir until the mixture starts to boil; do not scrape the sides of the pan. When the mixture starts to boil gently, reduce the heat to low and place a lid on the pot for 60 seconds. When time is up, remove the lid and let the mixture boil lightly, not uncontrollably, until it reaches a soft-ball stage, meaning that if a piece of the mixture were dropped into water, it would turn into a soft ball. Turn the heat off and add the semisweet chocolate chips, milk chocolate chips, vanilla, and marshmallows. Stir gently until all is melted. While the mixture is still hot, pour it into a glass or stainless-steel mixing bowl that has been sprayed with nonstick spray. Let it sit for 5 to 7 minutes until it cools slightly but is still hot. Then beat the fudge with an electric mixer for about 5 to 6 minutes, or until the fudge is glossy and smooth. Add the nuts and stir well. While the fudge still is hot, pour it into a 9 x 9-inch pan that has been sprayed with nonstick spray. Smooth the fudge out in the pan and let it sit and completely cool. Cut it into servings. The fudge will be smooth and soft.

◇◇◇◇◇◇◇◇◇◇◇◇◇◇◇◇◇◇◇◇◇◇

YIELD: 25 PIECES

CopyKat.com's **MRS. FIELDS®**

Pecan Pie Brownies

These are some unusual brownies—they don't have chocolate in them. They taste like pecan pie, and I like to take these somewhere like a picnic or to share at the office.

16 pecan halves

3 tablespoons dark corn syrup, divided

½ cup vegetable shortening

½ cup brown sugar

2 tablespoons molasses

¼ cup chopped pecans

2 egg yolks, beaten

1 teaspoon vanilla extract

1½ cups flour

1 teaspoon baking powder

¼ teaspoon baking soda

¼ teaspoon salt

Preheat the oven to 350°F (or 325°F if you'll be using a glass baking dish). Mix the pecan halves with 1 tablespoon of the corn syrup and set aside. Beat the shortening with the brown sugar until creamy. Add the molasses, 2 tablespoons corn syrup, and the chopped pecans and blend. Beat in the egg yolks and vanilla. In a separate bowl, combine the flour, baking powder, baking soda, and salt. Slowly mix the dry ingredients into the batter until all the ingredients are blended well.

Transfer the batter to an 8 x 8-inch greased baking pan. Arrange the pecan halves that have been mixed with the dark corn syrup on top of the batter. Bake for 25 to 30 minutes, until the top has browned and gives slightly when touched.

YIELD: 16 SERVINGS

Key Lime Pie

After a delicious steak dinner, what would be better than a refreshing Key lime pie? In this recipe, use Key limes if you can find them, but if you can't, the limes you normally find in the grocery store are fine. Stay away from bottled lime juices.

CRUST:
1 cup graham cracker crumbs (about 14 sheets of graham crackers)

2 tablespoons sugar

4 tablespoons unsalted butter, melted

FILLING:
3 large egg yolks

1 (14-ounce) can sweetened condensed milk

½ cup lime juice, freshly squeezed

2 to 3 drops green food coloring (optional)

FOR CRUST: Preheat the oven to 325°F. In a medium-sized bowl, combine the graham cracker crumbs and sugar and blend with a fork until the sugar is evenly distributed. Drizzle in the melted butter and continue to stir with a folk until the crumbs form a soft mass. Press the crumbs into a pie pan with the back of a measuring cup so the bottom and sides of the crust are even. Bake this crust in the oven for 15 minutes.

FOR FILLING: While the crust is baking, you can start the filling by placing the egg yolks into a bowl and mixing with an electric mixer until they are light yellow and creamy. Gently add in the sweetened condensed milk and the lime juice and blend until smooth. If you want, you can add a couple of drops of green food coloring; this isn't necessary for the taste, but this pie isn't naturally too green.

FOR ASSEMBLY: Pour the filling into the prebaked pie shell. Bake the pie for 30 minutes, until the center is set and the filling wiggles slightly when shaken. Allow the pie to cool to room temperature before placing it in the refrigerator. The pie should chill for 2 to 3 hours before serving.

YIELD: 8 SERVINGS

CopyKat.com's **PANCHO'S MEXICAN BUFFET™**

Sopapillas

★

Sopapillas are the final touch to many Mexican-style meals. As I child, I always loved going out for Mexican food because it meant finishing the meal with sweet sopapillas drizzled with honey. Sopapillas are always best enjoyed when they are hot and fresh. You may want to sprinkle the tops with cinnamon and sugar before drizzling them with honey. One warning: These are quite addictive.

4 cups all-purpose flour

1¼ teaspoons salt

3 teaspoons baking powder

3 tablespoons sugar

2 tablespoons shortening

1¼ cups milk

10 cups vegetable oil, for deep-frying

honey

Sift the flour before measuring it and sift it again with the salt, baking powder, and sugar. Cut in the shortening and add the milk to make a soft dough that's just firm enough to roll out. Cover the bowl and let the dough stand for approximately 30 minutes. Heat about 2 inches of oil in a frying pan to about 350°F. Roll the dough out to ¼-inch thick on a lightly floured board and cut it into diamond-shaped pieces, about 2 to 3 inches big. Add a few pieces of dough at a time to the hot oil so that the oil doesn't cool too quickly. Turn all the pieces over at once so they will puff evenly, then turn them back over to brown both sides. Drain on paper towels and repeat the process with the remaining dough. Serve with honey.

YIELD: 4 DOZEN SMALL SOPAPILLAS

Lemon Ice Box Pie

Making this classic pie is easy, and everyone will enjoy this tangy refreshing dessert. It's particularly good in the summer, as the lemon flavor is so refreshing. I highly recommend using fresh lemon juice rather than bottled; you'll have more subtle flavors that way.

CRUST:

1 (9-ounce) box yellow cake mix (like Jiffy Mix), prepared as directed (see note)

2 tablespoons granulated sugar

FILLING:

1½ cups sugar

5 tablespoons flour

½ teaspoon salt

2¼ cups whole milk

3 egg yolks

⅓ cup lemon juice

½ teaspoon vanilla extract

1 (8-ounce) container whipped topping (like Cool Whip)

lemon zest, for garnish

FOR CRUST: Preheat the oven to 275°F. Crumble the cooled prepared cake and measure 2 tablespoons of the crumbs. Reserve these for topping the pie. Measure 2 cups of crumbs; pat the crumbs lightly down when measuring. Place the crumbs in a small bowl and mix in the sugar. Spray a 9-inch pie pan with nonstick spray and pat the cake crumbs into the pie pan along the sides and on the bottom. Bake the pie crust for 7 minutes. Watch it carefully so the crumbs don't scorch. This process will help to lightly set the crust. When it's done, remove and cool the crust.

FOR FILLING: In a 2-quart saucepan, mix the sugar, flour, salt, and milk. While stirring constantly, bring the ingredients to a low boil over medium heat and cook for 2 to 3 minutes until the mixture becomes thick. Remove the pan from the heat. In a small bowl, beat the egg yolks and add ½ cup of the hot mixture and whisk them together. Place the saucepan back on the stove at a low heat and slowly pour the egg yolks into the filling while whisking. Add the lemon juice and vanilla to the filling and bring it to a soft boil and cook for 2 to 3 minutes longer. Whisking throughout the cooking helps to eliminate lumps. When the filling is thick, remove the pan from the heat and set it aside to cool down. The filling may be poured into the crust while it's still a little warm but not hot.

FOR ASSEMBLY: Pour the cool filling into the pie crust. Place the pie in the refrigerator for several hours to set and chill completely. When chilled, top the pie with whipped topping and sprinkle the reserved 2 tablespoons of cake crumbs over the top. For garnish, top with fresh lemon zest.

NOTE: If you cannot find Jiffy Cake mix, you can use a regular cake mix, but you will have twice as much crust as you need. Making two pies might be a solution.

◇◇◇◇◇◇◇◇◇◇◇◇◇◇◇◇◇◇◇◇◇◇◇◇◇◇◇◇◇◇

YIELD: 8 SERVINGS

Pecan Delight

This is a light and airy pie that's not too filling, but still packs lots of flavor. If you enjoy pecan pie, you'll enjoy this dessert.

⅓ cup pecans, chopped small

½ cup Ritz Crackers, finely chopped

1 teaspoon vanilla extract

¼ teaspoon cream of tartar

3 egg whites (about ⅓ cup), at room temperature

¾ cup sugar

¼ cup chopped pecans, for topping

1 (8-ounce) container whipped topping (like Cool Whip)

Preheat the oven to 350°F. Place the chopped pecan pieces and the Ritz crackers on a baking sheet and bake for 5 minutes. You want to lightly roast the nuts and crackers; they should be a light golden color. Watch them carefully so they do not burn. Remove them from the oven when golden and place on a paper towel until cool.

Add the vanilla and cream of tartar to the egg whites and beat with an electric mixer. Slowly add the sugar and continue to beat the egg whites until very stiff peaks form and the sugar is dissolved. Fold in the roasted pecans and crackers.

Lightly spray a 10-inch pie pan with a nonstick spray. Transfer the egg white meringue mixture to the pan and spread it out in a layer about 1-inch thick covering the bottom of the pan. Hollow out a little hole in the middle of the meringue half the size of half a dime; this will help the shell bake evenly. Preheat the oven to 275°F and bake the meringue for 1 hour. The meringue should not scorch, but it will turn light tan in color. Turn the oven off and let the shell dry in the oven for another hour. Remove the shell and cool. When the shell is cool, fill it with the whipped topping and sprinkle the pecan pieces on top. Place the pie in the refrigerator to completely chill before serving.

NOTE: The meringue will whip fluffier and be fuller when prepared at low humidity.

YIELD: 8 SERVINGS

CopyKat.com's **RUSSELL STOVER™**

Pecan Brittle

We have all tried crunchy, crisp peanut brittle before, and it is fantastic. Imagine it with pecans, which give a special flavor to this classic treat. Making brittle isn't difficult, so if you've never tried making hard candy, this is a great recipe to start out with.

1 cup sugar	2 teaspoons liquid butter flavoring
½ cup light corn syrup	
½ cup water	1½ cups chopped pecans
2 tablespoons butter	1 teaspoon baking soda
½ teaspoon salt	

In a heavy pot, stir together the sugar, corn syrup, water, butter, salt, and butter flavoring. Bring the mixture to a simmer on medium heat and place a lid on the pot for one minute, then remove the lid. This will steam all the sugar crystals on the side of the pot and they'll slide down into the mixture. Place a candy thermometer in the pan, and continue to cook on medium heat, stirring frequently, until the candy reaches a soft-crack stage, meaning that when the mixture is dropped into cold water, the candy will form threads that will not break. Add the nuts and mix through. Continue to cook until the mixture reaches a hard-crack stage, meaning that when the mixture is dropped into cold water, it will form threads that *will* break. Remove the pot from the heat and add the baking soda. The mixture will foam, but make sure you blend the baking soda into the candy completely. Pour the candy onto a nonstick cookie sheet or a lightly buttered baking sheet. Spread it to ¼-inch thick or less while the candy is still hot, because it will start to harden quickly. When the candy is set and cool, break it into pieces and store it in an airtight container.

YIELD: 1 POUND CANDY

Kahlúa® White Russian Brownies

Maybe you have heard of cream cheese brownies, or even zebra brownies before. This recipe combines chocolatey brownies, cream cheese, and Kahlúa®. Talk about decadent! The Kahlúa® gives a wonderfully rich coffee flavor and when you combine this with vodka, you have the perfect brownie for adults.

2 (3-ounce) packages cream cheese, softened

3 eggs

1½ cups sugar, divided

¼ cup vodka

1¼ cups flour, divided

6 tablespoons butter, divided

½ cup cocoa powder

¼ teaspoon salt

¼ teaspoon baking powder

¾ cup Kahlúa, divided

Preheat the oven to 325°F. Cream together the cream cheese, 1 egg, ¼ cup sugar, vodka, 2 tablespoons flour, and 2 tablespoons soft butter and set aside. In a separate bowl, sift the remaining flour and sugar and the cocoa powder, salt, and baking powder. Stir in the remaining butter and add ½ cup Kahlúa. Add the remaining eggs one at a time and mix well. Pour half of the cocoa mixture into a buttered and lightly floured 9-inch baking pan. Add the cream cheese mixture and cut lightly with a knife to swirl the two batters, then add the remaining cocoa mixture. Bake for about 30 minutes; the brownies are done when a toothpick is inserted and comes out clean (I personally like these a little underbaked). When cool, brush the top with the remaining Kahlúa.

YIELD: 16 SERVINGS

CopyKat.com's **SARA LEE®**

Pound Cake

★

This pound cake can be the base for Cracker Barrel Old Country Store's® Strawberry Shortcake (page 186), or it can go well with a cup of coffee. With this recipe, you won't need to head to your grocery store's freezer section for pound cake.

¾ cup sugar

½ cup unsalted butter, at room temperature

3 eggs

1 cup cake flour

2 tablespoons powdered milk

1 tablespoon corn syrup

juice of half a small lemon

¼ teaspoon salt

½ teaspoon vanilla extract

¼ teaspoon nutmeg

½ teaspoon baking powder

¼ teaspoon mace (optional)

Preheat the oven to 325°F. Cream the sugar and butter together until light and fluffy. Add the eggs one at a time and mix well. Add the flour, powdered milk, and corn syrup and mix until everything is well incorporated. Add the lemon juice, salt, vanilla, nutmeg, baking powder, and mace (optional). Make sure everything is well blended, and pour the mixture into a greased 9 x 5-inch loaf pan. Bake for 45 minutes, checking for doneness by inserting a toothpick into the center and seeing if it comes out clean. You almost want to underbake this.

YIELD: 12 SLICES

Crispitos

Also known as *buñuelos* in many Mexican restaurants, these are favorites around my house. All you need are some flour tortillas, a little cinnamon, and some sugar to make this dessert.

2 tablespooons cinnamon
½ cup sugar

2 cups vegetable oil, for deep-frying
10 flour tortillas

In a small bowl, mix together cinnamon and sugar very well and set aside. In a Dutch oven or large skillet, heat the oil to 350°F. If you do not have a thermometer, you can set the pot on medium-high heat, but be careful to watch that it doesn't get too hot and begin to smoke. Cut the tortillas into quarters and deep-fry 2 to 4 wedges at a time. Allow them to cook on one side for about 30 seconds or until golden brown, turn over, and repeat. When both sides are brown, take the tortillas out and place them on paper towels to drain. Repeat with the remaining tortillas. While the tortillas are draining, liberally sprinkle them with the cinnamon and sugar mixture. These are really great with honey.

YIELD: 5 SERVINGS

CopyKat.com's

White Chocolate Oreos®

You will see these in the grocery store around Christmas. They come in boxes that are specially wrapped and cost a lot of money. But they are easy to make at home, and best of all, you can decorate them any way you desire.

1 (16-ounce) package white melting chocolate

1 (18-ounce) package Oreo cookies

sprinkles, for decoration

mini chocolate chips, for decoration

colored sugar, for decoration

Melt the white chocolate in either a double boiler or in the microwave. When using a microwave, a glass bowl works the best. Heat the melting chocolate in several 30-second intervals, stirring well in between each heating. Once the chocolate flows freely and is completely melted, it's ready. When the chocolate is melted, use a spreader knife and spread the chocolate coating on one side of each Oreo, then decorate with toppings of your choice. You may also wish to dunk the Oreo cookie completely into the white chocolate, although this is more difficult because the dark crumbs may fall into the melted chocolate. Let the cookies cool on waxed paper.

YIELD: APPROXIMATELY 30 COOKIES

Breakfasts

There's nothing better than a hearty breakfast to start your day. For me, the weekends are the perfect time to make breakfast to enjoy with friends and family. Also included in this chapter are recipes that you can make ahead of time and enjoy througout the week, like muffins that you can bring to work that will impress your co-workers. I have also included recipes for luscious cinnamon rolls, a variety of pancakes, and savory egg dishes that will have everyone in your breakfast crowd covered.

Cinnamon Rolls

This recipe was originally adapted from one that a reader of CopyKat .com sent in. Since then, we have made additional modifications to tweak this sweet treat even more.

DOUGH:

1 cup warm water (105 to 115°F)

2 (¼-ounce) packets or 4½ teaspoons active dry yeast

²⁄₃ cup plus 1 teaspoon granulated sugar, divided

1 cup warm milk

²⁄₃ cup butter, melted

2 teaspoons salt

2 eggs, slightly beaten

7 to 8 cups all-purpose flour, or more if needed

FILLING:

1 cup melted margarine (I personally suggest using butter)

1¾ cups granulated sugar, divided

3 tablespoons ground cinnamon

1½ cups walnuts (optional)

1 cup raisins (optional)

FOR DOUGH: In a small bowl, mix together the warm water, yeast, and 1 teaspoon sugar and set aside. In a large bowl, mix the milk, the remaining ²⁄₃ cup sugar, melted butter, salt, and eggs; stir well and add the yeast mixture. Add half the flour and mix until smooth. Stir in enough of the remaining flour until the dough is slightly stiff (the dough will be sticky).

Turn the dough out onto a well-floured board and knead for 5 to 10 minutes. Place the dough in a well-buttered glass or plastic bowl, cover, and let rise in a warm place, free from drafts, until it has doubled in bulk, about 1 to 1½ hours.

When the dough has doubled, punch the dough down and let it rest for 5 minutes. Roll it out on a floured surface into a 15 x 20-inch rectangle.

FOR FILLING: Spread the dough with ½ cup melted margarine (or butter). Mix together 1½ cups sugar and the cinnamon, and sprinkle the mixture over the buttered dough. Sprinkle the top with walnuts and raisins, if desired (Cinnabon's rolls don't have them).

FOR ASSEMBLY: Roll the dough up jellyroll-style and pinch the edge together to seal it. Cut the roll into 12 to 15 slices. Coat the bottom of a 9 x 13-inch baking pan and an 8 x 8-inch square pan with the remaining ½ cup melted butter, then sprinkle them with the remaining ¼ cup sugar. Place the cinnamon roll slices close together in the pans. Cover the rolls with a towel, and let the rolls rise in a warm place until the dough is doubled in bulk, about 45 minutes.

Preheat the oven to 350°F. Bake for 25 to 30 minutes, or until the rolls are nicely browned. Serve with Cinnabon Cinnamon Roll Icing (page 213).

YIELD: 12 TO 15 CINNAMON ROLLS

CopyKat.com's **CINNABON®**

Cinnamon Roll Icing

You can make rich, creamy frosting with cream cheese, butter, and vanilla, just like Cinnabon® does. Please note that the key to this delightful frosting is whipping it for at least 12 minutes, so be prepared to sign someone up for mixer duty—not that it should be that hard!

1 pound margarine

2 (8-ounce) packages cream cheese

2 pounds (about 8 cups unsifted) powdered sugar

2 teaspoons lemon juice or 1 teaspoon lemon extract

2 teaspoons vanilla extract

Allow the margarine and cream cheese to reach room temperature, then beat them together in a bowl with a mixer. Slowly add in all the powdered sugar. Once all of the sugar is in the bowl, mix for at least an additional 12 minutes. When the icing is almost done, add in the lemon juice or extract and the vanilla.

YIELD: APPROXIMATELY 8 CUPS

CopyKat.com's CINNABON®

Stix®

Are you looking for that flavor of Cinnabon® but want something lighter? Or maybe you haven't tried making cinnamon rolls before, but you still want to do something like them. These cinnamon roll sticks are very easy to make, and you could make them with your kids. I highly suggest you use parchment paper or even waxed paper when making these; otherwise the baked sugar will crystallize onto your pan and make cleaning a chore.

> 1 (16-ounce) package puff pastry dough
> ½ cup sugar
> 1 tablespoon cinnamon

Allow the puff pastry dough to defrost according to the manufacturer's directions. Preheat the oven to 350°F. In a small bowl, combine the sugar and the cinnamon and mix well. Open the puff pastry dough and take out one sheet and unfold it onto a clean counter. Unfold the rectangle of dough so the long side is toward you.

Spray the puff pastry dough with some nonstick spray, and sprinkle on 2 tablespoons of the cinnamon-sugar mixer. Using a pizza cutter, cut the dough in half horizontally, then cut it vertically into 10 pieces. Twist each cut piece of dough 2 to 3 times before placing them onto the parchment-covered cookie sheet. Sprinkle on an additional 1 tablespoon of the cinnamon-sugar. Repeat the process with the other sheet of puff pastry. Bake the sticks for approximately 15 minutes, or until they're your desired toasted color.

You can serve these with a half-recipe of the Cinnabon Cinnamon Roll Icing (page 213).

YIELD: 8 SERVINGS

Ham and Egg Casserole

Do you ever look for a little variety in your breakfasts? I find breakfast a little difficult to cook, and if you are making eggs for a large group, it is hard to serve them all at once. This casserole is almost a complete breakfast, with eggs, ham, and cheese all baked together. If you like, add some toast.

1 slice sourdough bread

4 to 5 eggs (1 cup), beaten

¼ teaspoon salt

¼ teaspoon ground black pepper

¼ cup evaporated milk

⅓ cup lean, cooked smoked ham, diced (country-cured ham, if available)

½ cup shredded mild cheddar cheese

Spray a 2-quart casserole dish with a nonstick spray. Cut the crust off the bread and trim it to fit the bottom of the dish, then place the bread on the bottom of the casserole dish. In a bowl, beat the eggs and add the salt, pepper, and evaporated milk and mix completely. Pour the egg mixture over the bread. Sprinkle the diced ham over the egg mixture and cover the dish. Refrigerate the casserole overnight or for at least 5 hours.

Preheat the oven to 375°F. Remove the casserole from the refrigerator, spoon the shredded cheddar cheese into the dish, and gently smooth the cheese on top of the egg mixture. Bake for 20 to 22 minutes, depending on the depth of the casserole dish. The casserole is done when the eggs have set, so when you wiggle the dish, the eggs are firm.

YIELD: 8 SERVINGS

Hash Brown Casserole ✓

Is it even possible to have breakfast at the Cracker Barrel® without having this cheesy potato casserole? Honestly, this casserole is good for breakfast or at any meal.

½ cup (1 stick) butter

1 (2-pound) bag frozen country-style hash browns

½ cup finely chopped onion

seasoned salt, to taste (like Jane's Krazy Mixed-up Salt)

pepper, to taste

1½ to 2 cups Colby cheese, shredded (in this case, more is not necessarily better)

1 (10¾-ounce) can cream of chicken soup

Preheat the oven to 350°F. Melt the butter in a skillet, then add the hash browns and onions, and season with salt and pepper to taste. Cook until the hash browns are tender and brown. Set them aside. Mix together the cheese and the cream of chicken soup in a separate large bowl. Add the hash browns to the mixture, then transfer everything into a buttered 2-quart casserole dish and bake for 30 minutes or until golden brown.

YIELD: 12 SERVINGS

CopyKat.com's **DENNY'S®**

Chicken Fajita Skillet Breakfast

★

Tex-Mex food is wonderful, and I could eat it at every meal, every day. So leave it up to Denny's® to bring us a Tex-Mex breakfast. Grilled and seasoned chicken breasts along with all the other fajita goodness help give potatoes and eggs a real boost.

2 boneless skinless chicken breasts	4 eggs
1 teaspoon fajita seasoning	¼ cup half-and-half
1 small bell pepper, sliced	½ cup shredded cheddar cheese
1 small onion, sliced	½ cup sour cream (optional)
2 cups home fries or hash browns (leftovers or frozen and thawed)	½ cup guacamole (optional)
	salsa (optional)
salt and pepper, to taste	

Rub the chicken breasts with the fajita seasoning and let them marinate for 30 minutes, then slice the chicken into strips. Spray a hot skillet with nonstick spray and brown the chicken for about 5 to 7 minutes on each side; you want the chicken to be cooked through. Add the onion and bell pepper to the skillet and stir on high so they cook quickly. Remove the chicken, onions, and peppers from the pan, and set aside on a plate until the final assembly. In the same pan, brown the leftover cooked potatoes or use frozen, thawed hash browns, and cook them until they're as crisp as you desire. Add salt and pepper to taste. Divide the potatoes in half and place them on serving plates. In a bowl, mix the egg with the half-and-half and salt and pepper, to taste. In the same skillet you used for the potatoes, cook the eggs into two separate omelets. Place the omelets on top of the potatoes. Slice the cooked chicken breasts into bite-size pieces. Divide the cooked fajita chicken, onions, and peppers on top of the omelets. Sprinkle each omelet with ¼ cup cheese. Serve with sour cream, guacamole, and salsa, if you like.

YIELD: 2 LARGE SERVINGS

CopyKat.com's **DOLLY MADISON®**

Double Chocolate Chip Mega Muffin

Are you ever looking for a serious chocolate fix? With many different layers of chocolate, these muffins will live up to the task and satisfy your desire with a depth of chocolate flavor. These muffins are perfect for a weekend brunch, or even to save for later. They store well, and with 20 seconds in the microwave, you will have fresh-out-of-the-oven flavor all over again.

1 (18-ounce) package chocolate fudge cake mix

1 (3.4-ounce) package instant chocolate pudding

¾ cup water

4 eggs, beaten

½ cup vegetable oil

1 cup mini chocolate chips, frozen

¼ teaspoon almond extract

Preheat the oven to 350°F. Mix the cake mix, pudding mix, water, eggs, oil, and almond extract until smooth. Stir in the chocolate chips last and blend thoroughly.

Fill the cups of a muffin pan ¾ full and bake for 25 to 35 minutes until done, but do not overcook. This will depend on the size of the muffin cups. The muffins are done when a toothpick is inserted into the center of one and it is clean when pulled out. I like to make six very large muffins and 12 smaller ones for the timid.

YIELD: 1 DOZEN MUFFINS

CopyKat.com's IHOP™

Buttermilk Pancakes

Light and fluffy pancakes, piled high, are a wonderful way to start your day. You can make IHOP's™ signature dish at home, and you won't even have to wait for a table to enjoy these steaming hot pancakes.

1¼ cups flour	½ teaspoon baking soda
1½ teaspoons baking powder	1½ cups buttermilk
2½ teaspoons sugar	2 tablespoons vegetable oil
½ teaspoon salt	1 egg, slightly beaten

Combine the flour, baking powder, sugar, salt, and baking soda in a bowl. Add the buttermilk, oil, and egg. With a spoon, mix all the ingredients and beat until smooth.

Heat a frying pan or a griddle on medium-low heat. When the pan or griddle is hot, pour in a little oil or spray it with a nonstick spray. Pour in the batter to your desired-size pancake. Let the batter start to show small bubbles on top before you turn the pancake over to finish cooking. Turning pancakes is much easier if you spray your spatula with a nonstick spray so it does not stick to the uncooked dough of the pancakes when you are turning them. If the batter seems to be too thick, add a little more buttermilk, ⅛ to ¼ cup, and mix well.

YIELD: 9 (4 TO 5-INCH) PANCAKES

CopyKat.com's **IHOP™**

Colorado Omelet

If you like meat, you'll like this recipe. Ham, sausage, bacon, and roast beef are just a few of the ingredients that go into this hearty omelet. This is *so* hearty that you may want to enjoy it with a friend.

1 tablespoon butter

¼ cup diced sweet onions

¼ cup diced bell pepper

¼ cup diced cooked lean ham

3 to 4 eggs (1 cup), beaten

2 tablespoons water

¼ teaspoon salt

¼ cup diced tomatoes (optional)

1⅓ cups sliced small breakfast sausage links, fried and drained

¼ cup diced lean bacon, fried and drained

⅓ cup shredded roast beef or diced roast beef from the deli

¾ cup finely shredded cheddar cheese, divided

In a saucepan on medium-low heat, melt the butter and add the onions and bell peppers. Stir until the onions and peppers are soft but not browned. Add the diced ham and stir until the ham is softened and heated through. Immediately remove the pan from the heat and set aside.

In a mixing bowl, combine the eggs, water, and salt and beat well. Set aside.

Heat a 12-inch frying pan on medium-low heat, add a little oil (about 1 teaspoon) or spray it with a nonstick vegetable spray. A nonstick pan also works great. Place the egg mixture in the pan and sprinkle it with the cooked vegetables and ham. Add the tomato, if you wish, and sausage, bacon, half of the roast beef, and ½ cup of the shredded cheese. Place a lid on the pan until the omelet starts to set; depending on the heat of your stove, this should take just over a minute. Immediately remove the lid and fold the omelet from the sides to the middle. If this is difficult, fold it in half. Sprinkle the top with the rest of the cheese and roast beef. Serve with a side order of picante sauce or sour cream with a little diced green onion.

YIELD: 1 OMELET

Country Griddle Cakes

These are the pancakes just like the ones IHOP™ used to make, but they were recently removed from the menu—so you have to make them yourself! These pancakes have something extra: A little cream of wheat cereal makes them thick and dense. Looking for a morning treat that will really fill you up? These are your pancakes.

- 1½ cups flour
- 2 tablespoons sugar
- ½ teaspoon salt
- 2 teaspoons baking powder
- ½ teaspoon baking soda
- ¾ cup prepared cream of wheat, cooled (follow the directions on the box and cool before adding)

- 1½ cups buttermilk (plus ¼ cup more, if needed)
- 1 egg, slightly beaten
- 2 tablespoons vegetable oil

Combine the flour, sugar, salt, baking powder, and baking soda in a medium bowl. In a small bowl, mix the cream of wheat with the buttermilk, add the egg and stir to get any lumps out. Add the cream of wheat mixture to the dry ingredients. Stir the batter with a spoon until smooth. The batter may be a little lumpy.

Heat a grill or a frying pan on medium-low heat. When the surface is hot, lightly oil it or use a nonstick vegetable spray. Pour the batter into the pan to your desired size for pancakes and turn the pancakes when the tops have little bubbles. If you spray your spatula with a nonstick spray, it helps prevent the uncooked part of the pancake from sticking to the spatula, and flipping the pancake is much easier. If your pan is oiled well, your pancakes should not stick, and if the temperature is just right, your pancakes should have a beautiful golden color.

YIELD: 9 (4-INCH) PANCAKES

Breakfast Burrito

★ 🥩

Remember when McDonald's® used to cook more food in their restaurants? Growing up, I can remember the smell of the biscuits wafting through the air during breakfast. But as good as those biscuits were, I loved the breakfast burritos even more. This is the breakfast burrito as it used to be.

1 pound mild bulk pork sausage

½ cup diced yellow onion

1 tablespoon canned diced green chilies

¼ cup diced fresh tomatoes

9 eggs

10 to 12 (8 to 9-inch) flour tortillas

10 to 12 slices American cheese

your favorite taco sauce or picante sauce

sour cream (optional)

sliced avocado (optional)

Crumble and fry the pork sausage, stirring and separating the meat so it will fry in small little pieces. When the sausage is cooked, remove it from the heat, drain, and rinse it with hot water, then drain the water from sausage. Place the drained sausage in the frying pan and add the onion, green chilies, and tomatoes. Heat on medium temperature just until the sausage and vegetables are heated through, stirring frequently.

In a large bowl, beat the eggs. Add the eggs to the pan with the sausage mixture. When the eggs are cooked, remove them from the heat. In the middle of each flour tortilla, place one slice of cheese. Spoon one to two tablespoons of the egg mixture on to the tortilla and roll up the tortilla like you would a burrito or a wrap. Place the burritos on a platter, cover them with plastic wrap, and pop them in the microwave just long enough to heat and melt the cheese, about 1 minute at high power. Serve with your favorite taco or picante sauce. You will find these are mild and really great for breakfast. I like to add sour cream and a little avocado to mine. Cover and store the sausage and egg mixture that is not used and refrigerate. It will keep for several days for your next breakfast.

YIELD: 10 TO 12 SERVINGS

CopyKat.com's OTIS SPUNKMEYER™

Banana Nut Muffins

Intense banana flavor is what you're in store for with these very moist muffins that you'll be proud to serve. Lots of walnuts make these muffins disappear in no time.

1 cup mashed ripe banana (about 2 average-sized bananas)

1 (18-ounce) box banana cake mix

1 (3.4-ounce) box instant banana pudding

4 eggs

½ cup vegetable oil

¾ teaspoon ground cinnamon

½ cup water

1 teaspoon banana extract

1 cup finely chopped walnuts

Preheat the oven to 350°F. Blend all the ingredients together until smooth, mixing for about 3 to 4 minutes. Fill the cups of a muffin pan ¾ full and bake for about 20 minutes until done. Check for doneness by inserting a toothpick into the top of a muffin; if the toothpick comes out clean, the muffins are done. Store the muffins in an airtight container.

YIELD: 9 LARGE MUFFINS OR 12 SMALL MUFFINS

Blueberry Muffins

★ ▯

If the name says Otis Spunkmeyer™, you can't go wrong. These are tasty muffins. As a child, blueberry muffins were one of my favorites, and these muffins are nice and dense with wonderful blueberries bursting through, full of flavor.

1 (15-ounce) can blueberries in liquid

4 eggs

1 (18-ounce) package white cake mix

1 (3.4-ounce) package instant vanilla pudding (4-serving size)

½ cup vegetable oil

1 teaspoon vanilla extract

¾ cup milk

Preheat the oven to 350°F. Rinse the blueberries lightly and drain them well. In a mixing bowl, beat the eggs until light. To the eggs, add the cake mix, pudding mix, vegetable oil, vanilla, and milk. Beat until smooth but do not overbeat, about 2 to 2½ minutes. The batter will be thick. Carefully fold the blueberries into the batter with a spoon or spatula. Try not to break the berries, as they can be very tender.

Fill the cups of a muffin pan ¾ full and bake for 20 to 30 minutes, depending on the size of your muffin cups; do not overbake. Check for doneness by inserting a toothpick into the top of a muffin; if the toothpick comes out clean, the muffins are done. Store the muffins in an airtight container.

YIELD: 9 LARGE MUFFINS OR 12 TO 15 SMALL MUFFINS

CopyKat.com's **OTIS SPUNKMEYER™**

Spicy Corn Muffins

These corn muffins are unique. They are sweet and have a hint of spice, and they go perfectly with a bowl of chili. Everyone will wonder how you managed to get the sweet and spice together.

1 cup yellow cake mix

2 (8½-ounce) boxes Jiffy Mix Corn Muffin Mix

1 teaspoon salt

2 eggs, beaten

²/₃ cup milk

½ cup sour cream

¹/₃ cup vegetable oil

1 tablespoon finely diced jalapeño (canned; remove seeds before dicing)

2 tablespoons finely diced red bell pepper

Preheat the oven to 350°F. In a large mixing bowl, blend the cake mix, Jiffy Mix, salt, eggs, and milk. Add the sour cream and oil. Beat until the batter is mixed and fairly smooth. Fold in the jalapeños and bell peppers and mix them throughout the batter. Fill the cups of a muffin pan ¾ full (or use little loaf tins the size of muffin cups), and bake for about 20 to 25 minutes, or until done. Check for doneness by inserting a toothpick into the top of a muffin; if the toothpick comes out clean, the muffins are done. Store in an airtight container.

YIELD: 18 MUFFINS

Banana Walnut Bread ✓

It's such a treat to go into Starbucks™ and enjoy a coffee and something sweet. It is one of my life's little pleasures. Freshly baked banana bread is hard to beat, and it isn't difficult to make. Unlike in the store, you can enjoy this bread while it is still warm out of the oven. I recommend using bread flour if you have it on hand, as it gives the bread a denser feel. Why not try making some of this banana walnut bread to take to your co-workers?

1¾ cups flour (bread flour is best)

2 teaspoons baking powder

½ teaspoon baking soda

½ teaspoon salt

⅓ cup margarine (see note)

⅔ cup sugar

1 cup mashed ripe banana (from 2 or 3 bananas)

2 tablespoons milk

2 eggs

1 cup chopped walnuts, divided

Preheat the oven to 350°F. In a medium-sized bowl, combine the flour, baking powder, baking soda, and salt. In another medium-sized bowl, combine the margarine and sugar, and cream them with an electric mixer until light and fluffy. Add in the mashed bananas, milk, and eggs and mix well. Add half of the dry ingredients into the wet ingredients and mix until they are just combined. Then add in the remaining dry ingredients and ½ cup walnuts. Blend until everything is mixed together. Do not overmix.

Pour the batter into a greased 8 x 4-inch loaf pan. Top the batter with the remaining chopped walnuts. Bake for 55 to 60 minutes, or until a toothpick inserted near the center comes out clean. Cool for 10 minutes on a wire rack.

NOTE: While Starbucks does not make their banana bread with butter, I think it comes out richer this way. I also like to add in a sprinkle or two of cinnamon and sugar, which also is not in their recipe, but it adds that little something extra.

YIELD: 1 LOAF

Sauces and Dressings

Sauces and salad dressings are some of my favorite things to enjoy when I go out to eat. At home, we don't always go to the effort to make that extra sauce that we enjoy, but honestly, many of these sauces are really easy to make. You can turn an any-night-of-the-week dinner into something more by adding a special sauce. Included in this chapter are recipes for a horseradish sauce just like Arby's®, which would be perfect with roast beef. Want to make your own honey mustard to dip chicken tenders in? I have a recipe better than any honey mustard you can buy in the grocery store.

Horsey Sauce®

I personally love Arby's®. I will head there long before I will go to a fast-food burger place. This not-too-spicy sauce goes very well with roast beef or on a sandwich.

1 cup mayonnaise

1 teaspoon white vinegar

2 tablespoons prepared horseradish

1 (single serving) packet Equal

dash of salt

In a small bowl, combine all the ingredients and mix well. Cover the bowl with plastic wrap and place it in the refrigerator for two to three hours before serving.

YIELD: APPROXIMATELY 1 CUP

CopyKat.com's **ARBY'S®**

Sauce

Whenever I go to Arby's®, I always dip the fries into their special sauce. If you have never had it before, it's ketchup with a spicy kick. This flavorful sauce goes well on french fries, on a burger, or even on a steak. It's also a nice change on pastrami and makes a great dipping sauce for hot wings.

1 tablespoon cornstarch

1 cup plus 2 tablespoons water

½ cup ketchup

2 tablespoons brown sugar

¼ cup white vinegar

¾ teaspoon onion powder

¾ teaspoon garlic powder

½ teaspoon paprika

3 tablespoons Worcestershire sauce (like Lea & Perrins)

⅛ teaspoon salt

⅛ teaspoon cayenne pepper

Mix the cornstarch and 2 tablespoons water together well and set aside. Place the remaining 1 cup water, ketchup, brown sugar, white vinegar, onion powder, garlic powder, paprika, Worcestershire sauce, salt, and cayenne pepper in a blender and blend on high speed for 15 to 20 seconds. Pour all the ingredients into a small saucepan and heat on medium-low. Simmer gently for 20 minutes, stirring several times. After 20 minutes, add the cornstarch mixture and stir well. When the sauce begins to thicken, let it simmer on a very low temperature for 10 minutes. Remove the pan from the heat and let the sauce cool. The sauce will be similar in consistency to steak sauce. Store it in a covered container in the refrigerator.

YIELD: APPROXIMATELY 1¾ CUPS

CopyKat.com's **ARMSTRONG'S™**

Cheese Sauce

This creamy cheese sauce goes with Armstrong's™ Turkey Devonshire (page 94), but you can use it on many other favorites of yours as well. You may want to enjoy this cheese sauce on top of steamed broccoli or cauliflower, or even pour it over pasta for some quick-and-easy macaroni and cheese.

2 tablespoons butter	½ cup sharp cheddar cheese
2 tablespoons flour	salt, to taste
1¼ cups milk (I like to use a mixture of half-and-half and milk), heated	cayenne pepper, to taste
	paprika, to taste

Melt the butter in a saucepan on medium heat. Stir in the flour and cook, stirring constantly, until the paste cooks and bubbles a bit, but do not let it brown (if it browns, start over). This will take a couple of minutes. When the paste bubbles, add the hot milk. Stir continually and the sauce will begin to thicken. Bring to a low boil and add the cheese and salt. Add dashes of cayenne and paprika.

YIELD: APPROXIMATELY 2 CUPS

CopyKat.com's **CHILI'S®**

Awesome Blossom®
Dipping Sauce

This is a well-seasoned, flavorful sauce that goes well with Chili's®
Awesome Blossom® (page 34), but don't limit yourself to serving it
with that recipe only. Consider this sauce to be something new for
burgers, or enjoy it as a dipping sauce for french fries.

½ cup sour cream

2 tablespoons ketchup

½ teaspoon seasoned salt

⅛ teaspoon crushed red pepper

1½ teaspoons fresh horseradish

¼ teaspoon paprika

red pepper, for garnish

Mix all the ingredients together and serve the sauce in the middle of the
Awesome Blossom. Garnish with extra paprika and just a dash of red pepper
if you desire.

YIELD: APPROXIMATELY ¾ CUP

CopyKat.com's **CHINESE**

Hot Mustard

Who doesn't love a sauce that packs some heat? Chinese hot mustard is very easy to make and can be used in many different ways. Looking for something to serve at a cocktail party that would be more interesting than just another plain old dip? This may be the one for you. If you think this is too hot at first, wait a couple of days. Hot mustard loses heat over time.

¼ cup boiling water

¼ cup dry mustard
(like Coleman's)

½ teaspoon salt

2 teaspoons vegetable oil

Using a whisk, stir the boiling water into the dry mustard until smooth. Add the salt and oil and mix well.

YIELD: APPROXIMATELY ½ CUP

CopyKat.com's **CHINESE**

Sweet and Sour Sauce

Do you take lots of extra packages of sweet and sour sauce when you go out for Chinese food? I do. Now you can make your own sauce at home and enjoy a little sweet and sour sauce with anything you desire.

1 tablespoon cornstarch	2 tablespoons ketchup
1 cup plus 2 tablespoons water, divided	dash of salt
	dash of MSG
1/3 cup white vinegar	dash of white pepper
1/2 teaspoon Worcestershire sauce	dash of Tabasco
2/3 cup sugar	

Combine the cornstarch and 2 tablespoons water and set aside. In a saucepan, cook the vinegar over medium heat and add the cornstarch mixture and Worcestershire sauce. Cook until the sauce is bubbly and thick. Remove the pan from the stove and add the ketchup, salt, MSG, white pepper, and Tabasco. This will stay good in the refrigerator for about a week.

YIELD: APPROXIMATELY 1 CUP

CopyKat.com's **HERSHEY®'S**

Chocolate Syrup

Sometimes you are in a bind and really need some chocolate syrup. With this recipe, you can easily make your own chocolate syrup at home and have that chocolate sauce for your ice cream or chocolate milk.

½ cup cocoa powder
(Hershey's, obviously)
1 cup sugar
dash of salt

1 cup water
1 teaspoon vanilla extract

Combine the cocoa powder, sugar, and salt in a saucepan. Add the water and mix until smooth. Bring this mixture to a boil. Allow it to boil for one minute, but be careful that it does not boil over. Remove the syrup from the heat, and when it cools, add the vanilla.

YIELD: APPROXIMATELY 2 CUPS

CopyKat.com's **HOOTERS™**

Hot Wing Sauce

You can't have wings without sauce. If you don't feel like making wings, you can serve this spicy and slightly sweet sauce with chicken tenders, or anything else you like.

1½ cups butter, softened

½ cup plus 2 tablespoons Tabasco sauce

3 tablespoons brown sugar

¾ teaspoon paprika

¾ teaspoon salt

1 tablespoon balsamic vinegar

½ teaspoon cayenne pepper

2 tablespoons chili sauce

In a small bowl, whisk all the ingredients together until the texture is uniform. It may seem like this takes a while, but continue whisking and you will get a nice even mixture. This will store well in a covered container in the refrigerator for up to two weeks. Serve with the Hooters Hot Wings (page 109).

YIELD: APPROXIMATELY 2 CUPS

Buttermilk Garlic Salad Dressing

So often we get stuck using the same salad dressings over and over again. Looking for something that is creamy like a Ranch-style dressing but has a different flavor? This buttermilk garlic salad dressing may be just what you are looking for. It also goes very well with chicken tenders and even french fries.

2/3 cup sour cream

1 cup mayonnaise

1/4 teaspoon crushed garlic

1/2 teaspoon salt

1 teaspoon paprika

1/2 teaspoon freshly ground pepper

1 teaspoon dry mustard

2 tablespoons sugar

1/2 cup buttermilk

Combine all the ingredients in a small bowl and mix well. If you have a stick blender, this is a great way to mix up this salad dressing. Store the dressing in an airtight container. This is best made 4 to 6 hours before serving.

YIELD: APPROXIMATELY 2 CUPS

Honey Mustard Salad Dressing

All dishes served from the Houston's™ kitchens are high quality and always have a unique take on a recipe. Their honey mustard is different from many others with the additions of cider vinegar, garlic salt, and olive oil. Think of additional ways you can use this dressing other than just in salad, like as a vegetable dip, sandwich spread, or with chicken tenders.

1 cup olive oil	¾ cup Dijon mustard
¼ cup cider vinegar	dash garlic salt
1⅛ cups honey	¾ cup mayonnaise

Combine all the ingredients in a small bowl and mix well. Cover, and place in the refrigerator; allow the mixture to sit for at least 4 hours. This will keep for a couple of weeks in a covered container.

YIELD: APPROXIMATELY 3 CUPS

CopyKat.com's **JASON'S DELI™**

𝓕𝓻𝓾𝓲𝓽 𝓓𝓲𝓹

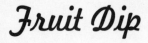

Serve this with fresh-cut fruit and you have a delicious snack. We are sure you'll want to enjoy more fruit with this quick and easy recipe. This dip stays fresh for about a week in the refrigerator.

> 1 cup sour cream
> ½ cup light brown sugar
> 4 teaspoons Grand Marnier liqueur

Whisk together all the ingredients in a medium bowl until the sugar is dissolved. Chill for an hour and stir again before serving; the alcohol can settle to the bottom and you want to mix it back into the dip.

YIELD: APPROXIMATELY 1¾ CUPS

Pineapple Dipping Sauce

If you like sweet and sour sauce, you will enjoy this doctored-up version. By adding crushed pineapple and red plum preserves, you can give premade sweet and sour sauce a completely new flavor.

1 (8-ounce) can crushed
pineapple in natural juice
(do not drain)

½ cup sugar

¼ cup red plum preserves

½ cup bottled sweet and
sour sauce

Place all the ingredients in a saucepan and simmer on medium-low to low heat for 20 to 25 minutes, stirring frequently, until the mixture thickens slightly. Serve with Joe's Crab Shack Coconut Shrimp (page 112).

YIELD: APPROXIMATELY 1½ CUPS

Barbecue Sauce

In Houston, Luther's™ was known for having really good barbecue. Their sauce was smoky, but not overly sweet. You can use our re-creation of it on brisket, ribs, chicken, and much more. This sauce will keep in the refrigerator for a week if you want to make some ahead of time that to enjoy later. If you are looking for a barbecue sauce that captures some of what makes Texas barbecue so delicious, this recipe is just what you need.

3 (8-ounce) cans tomato sauce

¼ onion, minced fine

½ cup brown sugar

1 teaspoon black pepper

½ teaspoon dry mustard

1 teaspoon salt

1 tablespoon molasses

1 tablespoon corn syrup

¼ teaspoon cayenne pepper

1 teaspoon garlic powder

2 to 3 teaspoons liquid smoke

Combine all the ingredients in a medium saucepan, mix well, and simmer for 1 hour over low heat.

YIELD: APPROXIMATELY 1¾ CUPS

CopyKat.com's **MASON JAR™**

Honey Mustard

Honey mustard can be used in so many ways. Everyone loves to dip their chicken tenders into it, and it can also work well as a salad dressing. I have even used this for making deviled eggs.

1 cup mayonnaise	1 teaspoon cider vinegar
¼ cup Dijon mustard	¼ teaspoon cayenne pepper

In a small bowl, whisk all the ingredients together. Chill this mustard for at least 1 hour before serving so the flavors can blend together.

YIELD: APPROXIMATELY 1¼ CUPS

Secret Sauce

Although this sauce goes well on a Big Mac®, it's also good on most any sandwich. India relish is a type of pickle relish, just like dill relish is a kind of pickle relish, but it has some extra spice in there to make it the perfect choice for this recipe. It can be found at your local grocery store.

1 cup mayonnaise

2 tablespoons India relish, drained

½ teaspoon granulated sugar

2 tablespoons Thousand Island dressing

Mix all the ingredients together. Let the sauce stand for at least 20 minutes, but allowing it to sit overnight is best.

YIELD: APPROXIMATELY 1¼ CUPS

Garlic Butter

The Original Pasta Company™, a Houston-area restaurant chain, would serve garlic butter and a loaf of fresh bread for you to nibble on before your meal came. I thought this garlic butter was very tasty, and made this recipe so I could have creamy garlic butter anytime.

½ cup butter

6 cloves garlic

½ teaspoon fresh parsley, minced

Allow the butter to reach room temperature. Peel the cloves of garlic and chop them fine. Stir the chopped garlic and parsley into the softened butter. You can place the butter into a mold if you like, or transfer it into a small container. This keeps up to a month in the refrigerator.

YIELD: APPROXIMATELY ½ CUP

Dipping Sauce

You can't serve Outback's™ Aussie Cheese Fries (page 51) without this specially spiced dipping sauce. This is also great with grilled chicken, chicken tenders, or even as a creative sauce on a hamburger.

1 (16-ounce) bottle
Ranch dressing

2 teaspoons paprika

1 teaspoon cayenne pepper

1 teaspoon dried thyme

1 teaspoon dried oregano

1 teaspoon white pepper

1 teaspoon black pepper

1 tablespoon kosher salt

1 tablespoon garlic powder

1 tablespoon onion powder

In a small bowl, combine all ingredients and mix well. This is best if allowed to refrigerate overnight.

YIELD: 2 CUPS

CopyKat.com's **OUTBACK STEAKHOUSE™**

Honey Mustard Dipping Sauce

The Outback Steakhouse™ makes a wonderful honey mustard dipping sauce, and what I really like about it is its consistency. I can't make chicken fingers without wanting to dip them into this sauce.

½ cup prepared yellow mustard	¼ cup mayonnaise
¼ cup honey	¼ cup light corn syrup, or to taste

Using a whisk, blend all the ingredients together until completely smooth and free of lumps. The corn syrup may be adjusted depending on how sharp the mustard might be, or to your taste.

◇◇◇

YIELD: APPROXIMATELY 1 CUP

Honey Mustard Salad Dressing

Honey mustard salad dressing is so versatile. You can use this on a salad, or to dip chicken tenders into, or even as a sandwich spread. This dressing is very easy to make, and after trying it once, you won't be purchasing any more honey mustard salad dressing in a jar.

1½ cups mayonnaise

¼ cup Dijon mustard (Grey Poupon is highly recommended)

½ cup honey

Combine all the ingredients in a bowl and mix well. Allow to set for at least 2 hours before serving; overnight is best.

YIELD: 2¼ CUPS

CopyKat.com's **OUTBACK STEAKHOUSE™**

Tiger Dill Sauce

This is the great stuff they serve with your steak at Outback™. I have always enjoyed this easy-to-make sauce as something different for your normal steak at home or for any other beef dish. This goes well over baked potatoes too!

²/₃ cup sour cream	¾ teaspoon sugar
3 teaspoons prepared horseradish (see note)	¼ teaspoon dried dill

In a small bowl, blend all the ingredients together. This is better if let to set overnight.

    NOTE: If your horseradish isn't as spicy as it used to be—it loses heat as it ages—taste the sauce and add more horseradish.

YIELD: APPROXIMATELY 1 CUP

Honey Mustard Dipping Sauce

At the Rainforest Cafe®, this sauce is served on the Caribou Coconut Chicken (page 129), but it can be used on a variety of meats and even salads. The cayenne pepper gives it a special kick, and this sauce will stay fresh for several days in the refrigerator.

> ⅓ cup honey mustard (like French's)
> ¼ cup mayonnaise
> ¼ teaspoon cayenne pepper

Mix the honey mustard, mayonnaise, and cayenne pepper together and blend well. Place in a covered container and refrigerate until ready to use.

YIELD: APPROXIMATELY ¾ CUP

CopyKat.com's **RED LOBSTER®**

Piña Colada Dipping Sauce

This is a delightful sweet dipping sauce perfect for shrimp or even chicken nuggets.

1 cup piña colada mix (Major Peters' is my favorite)

¼ cup plus 1 tablespoon cold water, divided

2 tablespoons crushed pineapple, drained

1 tablespoon plus 1 teaspoon sweetened coconut flakes

3 tablespoons plus 1 teaspoon powdered sugar

1½ teaspoons cornstarch

Mix the piña colada mix, ¼ cup water, crushed pineapple, coconut, and powdered sugar in a saucepan. Heat on medium-low temperature until the sauce begins to simmer, stirring frequently. Let the mixture simmer slowly for 10 to 12 minutes. Mix the cornstarch and the remaining water together, add it to the sauce, and blend well. Let the mixture simmer for 3 to 5 minutes longer, stirring. Remove the sauce from the heat and bring it to room temperature. Serve at room temperature with Red Lobster Parrot Isle Coconut Shrimp (page 132).

YIELD: APPROXIMATELY 1½ CUPS

Honey Butter

Bread always tastes better with sweet, creamy honey butter. Honestly, this butter goes well on any type of bread, not just the delicious beer bread they serve at Saltgrass Steak House™. You can put this on toast, muffins, or anything you desire. You don't have to make homemade bread just to have honey butter.

½ cup (1 stick) butter, softened
2 tablespoons condensed milk
¼ cup plus 1 tablespoon honey

In a small food processor or blender, whip the butter, milk, and honey until they turn a light cream color. This should take about 30 seconds. Shape the butter with a melon baller. Cover and refrigerate the balls until you're ready to serve. You may also omit the honey and serve with your Saltgrass Steak House Shiner Bock Beer Bread (page 166).

YIELD: APPROXIMATELY ¾ CUP

CopyKat.com's **STEAK AND ALE™**

Marinade

While Steak and Ale™ may no longer be around, you can still enjoy their steak with my special recipe. You can use this marinade on steaks and chicken. The pineapple juice adds a complex citrus flavor to meats.

3½ cups pineapple juice	½ cup red wine vinegar
1 cup soy sauce	¾ cup sugar
1 cup dry white wine	2 teaspoons finely minced garlic

Simply mix all the ingredients together. The meat of your choice can marinate in this liquid for up to 24 hours, then grill or pan-fry it. For a little extra flavor, add a little bit of butter to the pan if you are going to cook it in a skillet. Do not reuse the marinade.

YIELD: APPROXIMATELY 5½ CUPS

CopyKat.com's **SWEET TOMATOES**®

Tomato and Basil Salad Dressing

★ 🗄 ⏱

Do you ever want a salad dressing that is tangy and fresh? This tomato and basil dressing may be just what you are looking for. Actually, it is my favorite thing at Sweet Tomatoes®. Before I cracked this recipe and could make it at home, I was known to take out this salad dressing from the restaurant by the pint.

½ cup mayonnaise

½ cup sour cream

⅓ cup sweet chili sauce

⅛ cup sweet pickle relish

½ teaspoon paprika

½ teaspoon finely chopped basil leaves

¼ cup Real Bacon Bits (packed in a cup)

In a small bowl, combine all the ingredients together and stir well. When you measure the bacon bits, push them down into the cup so you fill it completely. Cover the bowl with plastic wrap and refrigerate it for at least 4 to 6 hours before serving. The dressing tastes best when you allow it to sit overnight in your refrigerator before use.

YIELD: APPROXIMATELY 1½ CUPS

Mild Sauce

Now there's no need to walk out of the restaurant with tons of little sauce packets in your pockets. This easy-to-make sauce is tasty on tacos, nachos, and even fried eggs in the morning. You may also want to use it to flavor ground meat for tacos instead of using a package of seasoning mix.

1 (8-ounce) can tomato sauce

⅓ cup water

1 tablespoon white vinegar

¼ teaspoon chili powder

1½ teaspoons cumin

1½ teaspoons dried minced onions

½ teaspoon garlic powder

½ teaspoon garlic salt

¼ teaspoon paprika

¼ teaspoon sugar

¼ teaspoon cayenne pepper

Combine all the ingredients in a saucepan and stir well. Simmer at a very low temperature for 15 to 20 minutes. Remove the pan from the heat and cool. This can be kept in the refrigerator for several days.

YIELD: 1 CUP

Recipe Index

Alice Springs Chicken (Outback Steakhouse), 127

Almond Shortbread Cookies (Keebler), 191

Aussie Cheese Fries (Outback Steakhouse), 51

Awesome Blossom (Chili's), 34

Awesome Blossom Dipping Sauce (Chili's), 231

Baby Carrots (Cracker Barrel Old Country Store), 149

Bacon Caesar Burger (Denny's), 108

Bacon Ranch Salad (Betty Crocker Suddenly Salad), 62

Bacon Wrapped Sea Scallops (Red Lobster), 54

Baja Bean Salad (Sweet Tomatoes), 73

Baked Potato Skins (T.G.I. Friday's), 56

Baked Potato Soup (Houston's), 78–79

Banana Nut Muffins (Otis Spunkmeyer), 223

Banana Walnut Bread (Starbucks), 226

Bananas Foster (Brennan's), 171

Barbecue Sauce (Luther's Bar-BQ), 240

Beef and Cheddar Spud (McAlister's Deli), 119

Biscuits (Cracker Barrel Old Country Store), 150

Black Beans (Chili's), 146

Blueberry Muffins (Otis Spunkmeyer), 224

Bourbon Chicken (Cajun Café), 99

Bread Pudding (Golden Corral), 188

Breakfast Burrito (McDonald's), 222

Broccoli and Cheese Soup (Black-eyed Pea), 76

Broccoli and Cheese Soup (Sweet Tomatoes), 88

Brownie Cheesecake Cups (Mrs. Fields), 197

Buffalo Chicken Sandwich (Bennigan's), 95

Buffalo Shrimp (Tortuga Coastal Cantina), 59

Buttermilk Garlic Salad Dressing (Houston's), 236

Buttermilk Pancakes (IHOP), 219

Cajun Rice (Popeye's), 161

Cajun Shrimp (Bubba Gump Shrimp Co.), 98

Cajun Shrimp (Red Lobster), 130

Canadian Cheese Soup (Houston's), 80

Cantina Queso (Pappasito's), 52

Cantina Salsa (Pappasito's), 53

Capellini Pomodoro (Olive Garden), 121

Capellini Primavera (Olive Garden), 122

Caribou Coconut Chicken (Rainforest Cafe), 129

Carrot Cake (Cracker Barrel Old Country Store), 181–82

Carrot Salad with Pecans (Cracker Barrel Old Country Store), 63

Cheddar Bay Biscuits (Red Lobster), 163

Cheese Sauce (Armstrong's), 230

Cheesecake (The Cheesecake Factory), 172–73

Cherry Chocolate Cobbler (Cracker Barrel Old Country Store), 183

Cherry Dessert Pizza (CiCi's), 178

Cherry Limeade (Sonic), 24

Chicken Casserole (Cracker Barrel Old Country Store), 105–106

Chicken Durango (Luby's), 116

Chicken Enchilada Soup (Chili's), 77

Chicken Fajita Skillet Breakfast (Denny's), 217

Chicken Madeira (The Cheesecake Factory), 100–101

Chicken Marsala (Olive Garden), 123

Chicken Tenders (Cracker Barrel Old Country Store), 107

Chili (James Coney Island), 81

Chili (Steak 'n Shake), 86

Chili (Wendy's), 92

Chinese Hot Mustard, 232

Chinese Sweet and Sour Sauce, 233

Chocolate Brownie Sundae (Chili's), 176

Chocolate Dessert Pizza (CiCi's), 179

Chocolate Syrup (Hershey's), 234

Cinnamon Roll Icing (Cinnabon), 213

Cinnamon Rolls (Cinnabon), 211–12

Clam Chowder (Red Lobster), 85

Clam Chowder (Sweet Tomatoes), 89

Coca-Cola Cake (Cracker Barrel Old Country Store), 184–85

Cocoa Mix (Swiss Miss), 26

Coconut Cream Pie (Luby's), 195–96

Coconut Shrimp (Joe's Crab Shack), 112

Coleslaw (Houston's), 66

Colorado Omelet (IHOP), 220

Cornbread (Boston Market), 141

Country Griddle Cakes (IHOP), 221

County Fair Funnel Cakes, 180

Crab Alfredo (Red Lobster), 131

Crab Dip (Joe's Crab Shack), 40

Creamed Spinach (Boston Market), 142

Crispitos (Taco Bell), 208

Crusted Chicken Romano (The Cheesecake Factory), 102

Decadent Walnut Chocolate Fudge (Mrs. Fields), 198

Dill Potato Wedges (Boston Market), 143

Dipping Sauce (Outback Steakhouse), 246

Double Chocolate Chip Mega Muffin (Dolly Madison), 218

Dumplings (Cracker Barrel Old Country Store), 151

Fettuccine Salad (Souper Salad), 72

Fire Bites (T.G.I. Friday's), 57

Five Way Chili (Steak 'n Shake), 87

Foccacia (Romano's Macaroni Grill), 164

Freckled Lemonade (Red Robin), 21

French Onion Soup (T.G.I. Friday's), 91

Fried Apples (Cracker Barrel Old Country Store), 152

Fried Mozzarella (Olive Garden), 45

Frijoles a la Charra (Pappasito's Cantina), 159

Fritos Chili Cheese Wrap (Sonic), 134

Fruit Dip (Jason's Deli), 238

Fruit Punch Jell-O Salad (Furr's), 64

Garlic Butter (Original Pasta Company), 245

Garlic Mashed Potatoes (Bennigan's), 139

Garlic Mashed Potatoes (Saltgrass Steak House), 165

Gourmet Popcorn (Almond Roca), 30

Green Beans (Cracker Barrel Old Country Store), 153

Grilled Chicken Salad (Mason Jar), 70–71

Ham and Egg Casserole (Cracker Barrel Old Country Store), 215

Ham and Swiss Spirals (Nan's), 43

Hash Brown Casserole (Cracker Barrel Old Country Store), 216

Honey BBQ Strips (KFC), 114

Honey Butter (Saltgrass Steak House), 251

Honey Glazed Ham (Logan Farms), 115

Honey Mustard (Mason Jar), 241

Honey Mustard Dipping Sauce (Outback Steakhouse), 247

Honey Mustard Dipping Sauce (Rainforest Cafe), 248

Honey Mustard Salad Dressing (Houston's), 237

Honey Mustard Salad Dressing (Outback Steakhouse), 248

Honey-Butter Biscuits (Church's Chicken), 148

Horsey Sauce (Arby's), 228

Hot Artichoke Dip (Olive Garden), 46

Hot Wing Sauce (Hooters), 235

Hot Wings (Hooters), 109

Italian Chicken Breast (Luby's), 117

Jack Daniel's Grill Glaze (T.G.I. Friday's), 137

Kahlúa White Russian Brownies (Sara Lee), 206

Key Lime Pie (Outback Steakhouse), 200

Krab Salad (Alberstons), 61

Lemon Ice Box Pie (Piccadilly Cafeteria), 202–203

Lime Jell-O Salad (Furr's), 65

Macaroni and Cheese (Boston Market), 144

Macaroni and Cheese (Luby's), 156

Mac-A-Roo 'N Cheese (Outback Steakhouse), 157

Margarita Grilled Chicken (Chili's), 103

Marshmallow Rice Krispies Shake (Jack in the Box), 17

Mashed Potatoes (Cracker Barrel Old Country Store), 154

Meatloaf (Boston Market), 97

Mesquite Chicken (Mason Jar), 118

Mexican Grill Cilantro Rice (Chipotle), 147

Mexican Grill Guacamole (Chipotle), 37

Mexican Pizza (Taco Bell), 135

Mighty High Ice Cream Pie (Chili's), 177

Mild Sauce (Taco Bell), 253

Mini Buffalo Chicken Sandwiches (Jack in the Box), 110

Mini Sirloin Burgers (Jack in the Box), 111

Monte Cristo Sandwich (Bennigan's), 96

Monterey Chicken (Chili's), 104

Mudslide (Kahlúa), 20

Nine-Layer Dip (T.G.I. Friday's), 58

One Hour in the Candy Store (T.G.I. Friday's), 27

Onion Rings (Dairy Queen), 155

Onion Rings (Sonic), 168

Oreo Cheesecake (The Cheesecake Factory), 174–75

Painkiller (Soggy Dollar Bar), 23

Parmesan-Crusted Chicken Breast and Bow-Tie Pasta (Olive Garden), 124–125

Parrot Isle Coconut Shrimp (Red Lobster), 132

Pasta Alfredo (Olive Garden), 120

Pecan Brittle (Russell Stover), 205

Pecan Delight (Piccadilly Cafeteria), 204

Pecan Pie Brownies (Mrs. Fields), 199

Pecan Sandies (Keebler), 192

Pico de Gallo (Applebee's), 31

Piña Colada Dipping Sauce (Red Lobster), 251

Pineapple Dipping Sauce (Joe's Crab Shack), 239

Pizza Cinna Stix (Domino's), 187

Popcorn Shrimp (Joe's Crab Shack), 113

Potato Wedges (Bennigan's), 33

Pound Cake (Sara Lee), 207

Queensland Chicken and Shrimp (Outback Steakhouse), 128

Quesadillas (Applebee's), 32

Red Beans (Popeye's), 162

Red Hot Sauce (Ninfa's), 44

Rice Pudding (Kozy Shack), 193

Salsa (Chili's), 35

Sam Remo Dip (Olive Garden), 47

Sauce (Arby's), 229

Sautéed Shrooms (Outback Steakhouse), 158

Seasoned Meat (Taco Bell), 136

Secret Passion Punch (Joe's Crab Shack), 18

Secret Sauce (McDonald's), 242

Sex on the Beach (T.G.I. Friday's), 28

Shiner Bock Beer Bread (Saltgrass Steak House), 166

Shredded Carrot Salad (Luby's), 69

Shrimp Christopher (Olive Garden), 126

Shrimp Scampi (Red Lobster), 133

Sicilian Scampi (Olive Garden), 48

Simple Beer Bread, 167

Skillet Queso (Chili's), 36

Smurf Punch (Ruby Tuesday), 22

Sopapillas (Pancho's Mexican Buffet), 201

Southwest Caesar Salad (Houston's), 67–68

Spicy Corn Muffins (Otis Spunkmeyer), 225

Spinach Artichoke Dip (Houston's), 39

Squash Casserole (Black-eyed Pea), 140

Steak and Ale Marinade, 251

Stix (Cinnabon), 214

Strawberries Romanoff (La Madeleine), 194

Strawberry Shortcake (Cracker Barrel Old Country Store), 186

Stuffed Jalapeños (Luby's), 41

Stuffed Mushrooms (Olive Garden), 49

Sugar and Spice Pecans, 55

Sweet Carrot Pudding (Piccadilly Cafeteria), 160

Sweet Potato Casserole (Boston Market), 145

Sweet Tea, 25

Tex-Mex Queso (Monterey's Little Mexico), 42

Three Bean Salad (Sweet Tomatoes), 74

Tiger Dill Sauce (Outback Steakhouse), 249

Toasted Ravioli (Olive Garden), 50

Toffee Pretzels (Crunch 'n Munch), 38

Tomato and Basil Salad Dressing (Sweet Tomatoes), 252

Tomato and Onion Soup (Sweet Tomatoes), 90

Turkey Devonshire (Armstrong's), 94

Turtle Pie (Baskin-Robbins), 170

Walkabout Creamy Onion Soup (Outback Steakhouse), 83–84

Walnut Apple Cobbler (Houston's), 189–90

White Chocolate Oreos, 209

Ya Ya Punch (Joe's Crab Shack), 19

Zuppa Toscana (Olive Garden), 82

Recipe Index

by Restaurant

ALBERSTONS™
Krab Salad, 61

ALMOND ROCA®
Gourmet Popcorn, 30

APPLEBEE'S®
Pico de Gallo, 31
Quesadillas, 32

ARBY'S®
Horsey Sauce, 228
Sauce, 229

ARMSTRONG'S™
Cheese Sauce, 230
Turkey Devonshire, 94

BASKIN-ROBBINS®
Turtle Pie, 170

BENNIGAN'S™
Buffalo Chicken Sandwich, 95
Garlic Mashed Potatoes, 139
Monte Cristo Sandwich, 96
Potato Wedges, 33

BETTY CROCKER®
SUDDENLY SALAD®
Bacon Ranch Salad, 62

BLACK-EYED PEA™
Broccoli and Cheese Soup, 76
Squash Casserole, 140

BOSTON MARKET®
Cornbread, 141
Creamed Spinach, 142
Dill Potato Wedges, 143
Macaroni and Cheese, 144
Meatloaf, 97
Sweet Potato Casserole, 145

BRENNAN'S™
Bananas Foster, 171

BUBBA GUMP SHRIMP CO.™
Cajun Shrimp, 98

CAJUN CAFÉ™
Bourbon Chicken, 99

THE CHEESECAKE FACTORY®
Cheesecake, 172–73
Chicken Madeira, 100–101

Crusted Chicken Romano, 102
Oreo Cheesecake, 174–75

CHILI'S®
Awesome Blossom, 34
Awesome Blossom Dipping Sauce, 231
Black Beans, 146
Chicken Enchilada Soup, 77
Chocolate Brownie Sundae, 176
Margarita Grilled Chicken, 103
Mighty High Ice Cream Pie, 177
Monterey Chicken, 104
Salsa, 35
Skillet Queso, 36

CHIPOTLE MEXICAN GRILL™
Cilantro Rice, 147
Guacamole, 37

CHURCH'S CHICKEN®
Honey-Butter Biscuits, 148

CICI'S™
Cherry Dessert Pizza, 178
Chocolate Dessert Pizza, 179

CINNABON®
Cinnamon Roll Icing, 213
Cinnamon Rolls, 211–12
Stix, 214

CRACKER BARREL OLD COUNTRY STORE®
Baby Carrots, 149
Biscuits, 150
Carrot Cake, 181–82
Carrot Salad with Pecans, 63
Cherry Chocolate Cobbler, 183

Chicken Casserole, 105–106
Chicken Tenders, 107
Coca-Cola Cake, 184–85
Dumplings, 151
Fried Apples, 152
Green Beans, 153
Ham and Egg Casserole, 215
Hash Brown Casserole, 216
Mashed Potatoes, 154
Strawberry Shortcake, 186

CRUNCH 'N MUNCH™
Toffee Pretzels, 38

DAIRY QUEEN®
Onion Rings, 155

DENNY'S®
Bacon Caesar Burger, 108
Chicken Fajita Skillet Breakfast, 217

DOLLY MADISON®
Double Chocolate Chip Mega Muffin, 218

DOMINO'S®
Pizza Cinna Stix, 187

FURR'S™
Fruit Punch Jell-O Salad, 64
Lime Jell-O Salad, 65

GOLDEN CORRAL®
Bread Pudding, 188

HERSHEY®'S
Chocolate Syrup, 234

HOOTERS™
Hot Wing Sauce, 235
Hooters Hot Wings, 109

HOUSTON'S™
Baked Potato Soup, 78–79
Buttermilk Garlic Salad Dressing, 236
Canadian Cheese Soup, 80
Coleslaw, 66
Honey Mustard Salad Dressing, 237
Southwest Caesar Salad, 67–68
Spinach Artichoke Dip, 39
Walnut Apple Cobbler, 189–90

IHOP®
Buttermilk Pancakes, 219
Colorado Omelet, 220
Country Griddle Cakes, 221

JACK IN THE BOX®
Marshmallow Rice Krispies Shake, 17
Mini Buffalo Chicken Sandwiches, 110
Mini Sirloin Burgers, 111

JAMES CONEY ISLAND™
Chili, 81

JASON'S DELI™
Fruit Dip, 238

JOE'S CRAB SHACK™
Coconut Shrimp, 112
Crab Dip, 40
Pineapple Dipping Sauce, 239
Popcorn Shrimp, 113
Secret Passion Punch, 18
Ya Ya Punch, 19

KAHLÚA®
Mudslide, 20

KEEBLER®
Almond Shortbread Cookies, 191
Pecan Sandies, 192

KFC®
Honey BBQ Strips, 114

KOZY SHACK®
Rice Pudding, 193

LA MADELEINE™
Strawberries Romanoff, 194

LOGAN FARMS®
Honey Glazed Ham, 115

LUBY'S™
Chicken Durango, 116
Coconut Cream Pie, 195–96
Italian Chicken Breast, 117
Macaroni and Cheese, 156
Shredded Carrot Salad, 69
Stuffed Jalapeños, 41

LUTHER'S BAR-BQ™
Barbecue Sauce, 240

MASON JAR™
Grilled Chicken Salad, 70–71
Honey Mustard, 241
Mesquite Chicken, 118

MCALISTER'S®
Deli Beef and Cheddar Spud, 119

MCDONALD'S®
Breakfast Burrito, 222
Secret Sauce, 242

MONTEREY'S LITTLE MEXICO™
Tex-Mex Queso, 42

MRS. FIELDS®
Brownie Cheesecake Cups, 197
Decadent Walnut Chocolate Fudge, 198
Pecan Pie Brownies, 199

NAN'S™
Ham and Swiss Spirals, 43

NINFA'S™
Red Hot Sauce, 44

OLIVE GARDEN®
Capellini Pomodoro, 121
Capellini Primavera, 122
Chicken Marsala, 123
Fried Mozzarella, 45
Hot Artichoke Dip, 46
Parmesan-Crusted Chicken Breast and
  Bow-Tie Pasta, 124–125
Pasta Alfredo, 120
Sam Remo Dip, 47
Shrimp Christopher, 126
Sicilian Scampi, 48
Stuffed Mushrooms, 49
Toasted Ravioli, 50
Zuppa Toscana, 82

ORIGINAL PASTA COMPANY™
Garlic Butter, 245

OTIS SPUNKMEYER®
Banana Nut Muffins, 223
Blueberry Muffins, 224
Spicy Corn Muffins, 225

OUTBACK STEAKHOUSE™
Alice Springs Chicken, 127
Aussie Cheese Fries, 51
Dipping Sauce, 246
Honey Mustard Dipping Sauce, 247
Honey Mustard Salad Dressing, 248
Key Lime Pie, 200
Mac-A-Roo 'N Cheese, 157
Queensland Chicken and Shrimp,
  128
Sautéed Shrooms, 158
Tiger Dill Sauce, 249
Walkabout Creamy Onion Soup,
  83–84

PANCHO'S MEXICAN BUFFET™
Sopapillas, 201

PAPPASITO'S CANTINA™
Frijoles a la Charra, 159
Queso, 52
Salsa, 53

PICCADILLY CAFETERIA™
Lemon Ice Box Pie, 202–203
Pecan Delight, 204
Sweet Carrot Pudding, 160

POPEYE'S®
Cajun Rice, 161
Red Beans, 162

RAINFOREST CAFE®
Caribou Coconut Chicken, 129
Honey Mustard Dipping Sauce, 248

RED LOBSTER®
Bacon Wrapped Sea Scallops, 54
Cajun Shrimp, 130
Cheddar Bay Biscuits, 163
Clam Chowder, 85
Crab Alfredo, 131
Parrot Isle Coconut Shrimp, 132
Piña Colada Dipping Sauce, 251
Shrimp Scampi, 133

RED ROBIN®
Freckled Lemonade, 21

ROMANO'S MACARONI GRILL™
Foccacia, 164

RUBY TUESDAY™
Smurf Punch, 22

RUSSELL STOVER®
Pecan Brittle, 205

SALTGRASS STEAK HOUSE®
Garlic Mashed Potatoes, 165
Honey Butter, 251
Shiner Bock Beer Bread, 166

SARA LEE®
Kahlúa White Russian Brownies, 206
Pound Cake, 207

SOGGY DOLLAR BAR™
Painkiller, 23

SONIC®
Cherry Limeade, 24
Fritos Chili Cheese Wrap, 134
Onion Rings, 168

SOUPER SALAD™
Fettuccine Salad, 72

STARBUCKS™
Banana Walnut Bread, 226

STEAK 'N SHAKE™
Chili, 86
Five Way Chili, 87

STEAK AND ALE™
Marinade, 251

SWEET TOMATOES®
Baja Bean Salad, 73
Broccoli and Cheese Soup, 88
Clam Chowder, 89
Three Bean Salad, 74
Tomato and Basil Salad Dressing, 252
Tomato and Onion Soup, 90

SWISS MISS®
Cocoa Mix, 26

T.G.I. FRIDAY'S®
Sex on the Beach, 28
Baked Potato Skins, 56
Fire Bites, 57
French Onion Soup, 91

Jack Daniel's Grill Glaze, 137
Nine-Layer Dip, 58
One Hour in the Candy Store, 27

TACO BELL®
Crispitos, 208
Mexican Pizza, 135
Mild Sauce, 253
Taco Bell Seasoned Meat, 136

TORTUGA COASTAL CANTINA™
Buffalo Shrimp, 59

WENDY'S®
Chili, 92

MISCELLANEOUS
Chinese Hot Mustard, 232
Chinese Sweet and Sour Sauce, 233
County Fair Funnel Cakes, 180
Simple Beer Bread, 167
Sugar and Spice Pecans, 55
Sweet Tea, 25
White Chocolate Oreos, 209

Other Ulysses Press Books

THE 100 BEST VEGAN BAKING RECIPES: AMAZING COOKIES, CAKES, MUFFINS, PIES, BROWNIES AND BREADS

Kris Holechek, $12.95

From classic breads, cakes, and desserts to imaginative new creations, the recipes in this book eliminate the dairy and eggs without reducing the flavor. These homemade delights have been taste-tested to tantalizing perfection.

THE I LOVE TRADER JOE'S COOKBOOK: OVER 150 DELICIOUS RECIPES USING ONLY FOODS FROM THE WORLD'S GREATEST GROCERY STORE

Cherie Mercer Twohy, $17.95

Based on the author's wildly popular, standing-room-only workshops, *The I Love Trader Joe's Cookbook* presents her top recipes for everything from crowd-pleasing hors d'oeuvres and tasty quick meals to gourmet entrées and world-class desserts.

THE I LOVE TRADER JOE'S PARTY COOKBOOK: DELICIOUS RECIPES AND ENTERTAINING IDEAS USING ONLY FOODS AND DRINKS FROM THE WORLD'S GREATEST GROCERY STORE

Cherie Mercer Twohy, $17.95

The ultimate one-stop party guide where everything's from Trader Joe's. With 50 party ideas from boozy to formal, this book offers easy-to-make and affordable recipes for each party, including hors d'oeuvres, gourmet entrées, hard drinks, wine advice, and desserts.

SUGAR-FREE GLUTEN-FREE BAKING AND DESSERTS: RECIPES FOR HEALTHY AND DELICIOUS COOKIES, CAKES, MUFFINS, SCONES, PIES, PUDDINGS, BREADS AND PIZZAS

Kelly Keough, $14.95

This book shows readers how to bring taboo treats back to the baking sheet with savory recipes that swap wheat for wholesome alternatives like quinoa, arrowroot, and tapioca starch, and trade in sugar for natural sweeteners like agave, yacon, and stevia.

WHO YOU CALLIN' CUPCAKE?: 75 IN-YOUR-FACE RECIPES THAT REINVENT THE CUPCAKE

Michelle and Vinny Garcia, $15.95

Sick and tired of the same-old, play-it-safe cupcake options? *Who You Callin' Cupcake?*, written by the master chefs of Chicago's popular Bleeding Heart Bakery, shows inspired bakers how to create delicious alternatives that will rock their guests.

To order these books call 800-377-2542 or 510-601-8301, fax 510-601-8307, e-mail ulysses@ulyssespress.com, or write to Ulysses Press, P.O. Box 3440, Berkeley, CA 94703. All retail orders are shipped free of charge. California residents must include sales tax. Allow two to three weeks for delivery.

About the Author

✕✕✕✕✕✕✕✕✕✕✕✕✕✕✕✕✕✕✕✕✕✕✕✕

Stephanie Manley is the creator and author of CopyKat.com. Since 1995, she has written recipes for restaurant-style dishes that anyone can make in their own kitchen. While working in restaurants, Stephanie began to write restaurant-style recipes to help save money and stretch her budget. Like many people, she couldn't afford to go out for dinner every night of the week, but wanted to re-create the taste of her favorite dishes at home. CopyKat.com, known for its trustworthy and delicious recipes, is now one of the internet's most popular cooking websites, and has been featured in publications like the *Wall Street Journal*, *Newsweek*, and *Woman's World*. Find Stephanie online at www.CopyKat.com or www.twitter .com/CopyKatRecipes. She lives in Kingwood, Texas.